300

To

Roz and Larry

for Friendship

Sherum

14 December 1997

STAYING SANE
IN A CRAZY WORLD

STAYING SANE
IN A CRAZY WORLD

Sherwin T. Wine

THE CENTER FOR NEW THINKING

Library of Congress Catalog Card Number: 95-092435

Publisher's Cataloging in Publication
Wine, Sherwin T.
    Staying sane in a crazy world : a guide to rational living /
Sherwin T. Wine
      p. cm.
      ISBN 0-9648016-0-4
      I. Conduct of life. 2. Reason. 3. Rationalism. I. Title.
BJ1581.2.W56 1995   170'.44
                                        QB195-20653

ISBN 0-9648016-0-4

CONTENTS

PREAMBLE

I am a believer.

But I am not a believer in a conventional sense.

I believe that we live in a crazy world, that there is no guarantee that the good will be rewarded and that the wicked will be punished.

I believe that the strength to cope with a crazy world comes from within ourselves, from the undiscovered power we have to look reality in the face and to go on living.

I believe that the best faith is faith in oneself, and that the sign of this faith is that we allow our reasoning mind to discipline our action.

I believe that the love of life means the love of reason and the love of beauty.

I believe that staying sane in a crazy world is not easy, but that in the long run, it is the foundation of our survival and self-esteem.

I believe that human dignity comes from the courage to live with reality and to enjoy its challenge.

PREFACE

Writing this book is a culmination of many years of public lectures at the Center for New Thinking and my congregation, The Birmingham Temple. The focus of many hours of my presentations has been the problem of living in a world which is not always kind or cooperative. Since I believe that being rational is essential to human happiness and human dignity, I have sought to help people deal more realistically with their frustrations and their expectations.

This book is intended to be both philosophic and pragmatic. Without real problems, philosophy is idle speculation. And without an overview, we cannot distinguish between what is important and what is trivial in life. Staying sane in a crazy world needs practical wisdom.

In completing this work I relied on the special devotion of my assistants Janice Leadbitter and Susie Sherman and on the extraordinary talents and enthusiasm of my friend Susan Levin. I am very grateful to them.

Sherwin Wine

REASON

This book is about the importance of being rational.

Being rational is no longer fashionable. Over the past forty years, writers, intellectuals and popular culture have turned against reason. They have held it up to public scrutiny, found it wanting and mocked it. Today the fashionable search is for the spiritual. From the revival of traditional religion to the popularity of New Age thinking, from the success of the new astrology to the search for cosmic consciousness, people, all over the world, are looking for answers to life's most vexing questions from the new gurus of intuition.

The traditional clergy have always attacked reason. But today they have been joined by their former enemies. Repentant intellectuals of the Left, and even political radicals, express regret over their former enthusiasm for reason and offer their tribute to the spiritual search. Most men and women who still admit to being rationalists, are aging and timidly defensive. They feel that they are standing on the last barricades and are bewildered by the assault. At a time when the world is fascinated with the creations of science and technology, the search for religion and spirituality is growing.

The assault on reason varies with the attacker. But there are some common themes. Reason is cold, dispassionate and unemotional, attuned to the narrow vision of the intellect and not to the wisdom of the heart. Reason is the product of the conscious mind, with all its screening out of the fine details of reality which the older, unconscious mind embraces. Reason is a function of the analytic powers of the left brain and is divorced from the synthetic powers of the right brain, where a deep ancient intuitive understanding of the universe finds its home. Reason is obsessed with discovering an objective reality and is indifferent to the internal subjective realities of the human spirit. Reason is attached to the arid procedures of logic and is not open to the bold intuitive leaps that defy syllogism and provide the genuine foundation for the revelation of truth. Reason is the prisoner of words and cannot deal with those fundamental mysteries that defy description.

And so it goes on endlessly, a free-for-all of continuous fault finding. Reason has become a "straw man" for the modern spiritualist movements. This status is quite a come down for a truth procedure that at one time enjoyed supremacy in the world of the professional and the educated. In the eighteenth and nineteenth centuries reason reigned supreme. Religion was on the defensive. Realities designated as spiritual, were suspected of being frauds. Even the clergy sought to hang their belief systems on the coat tails of reason. The Age of the Enlightenment and the Age of Science were hailed as the beginning of the messianic redemption of the human race. Rationalists felt powerful and put everyone else on the defensive.

But times have changed dramatically since the end of World War II. In a world of fading optimism, the faults of triumphant reason were exposed to public view. Reason was obviously naive about human progress. The horrors of war and holocaust hardly seemed to reflect the victory of human rationality. It was clearly off the mark with its touting of education and science. Both the educated and the scientific offered their allegiance to the banners of totalitarian fascism. It was ironically insensitive to its penchant for dogmatism. The ranting and ravings of Marxist "scientific socialists" about the virtues of dictatorship and censorship were embarrassing realities.

Two alternatives were possible. One was the admission that most so called rationalists had not been rational, that their naivety and dogmatism were inconsistent with reason. A radical revision of how reason presented itself to the world was required. Someone was needed to present a more authentic rational vision.

The other alternative was to demote reason and to search for another approach to truth and reality. Out of this option the spirituality movement was born (or revived in its contemporary form). For the first two decades after the War it grew slowly. But the trauma of the Vietnam debacle, its social upheavals, and the deep distrust of scientific establishments that emerged from it, fed its growth on the Left. Its strength on the Right was reinforced by the deep suspicion that atheism, Communism and reason all went together. Today it stands triumphant all over the world. Both liberals and conservatives drink from the fountains of "spiritual wisdom". The old rationalism is still being denounced. And a meaningful life is inconceivable without its "spiritual" dimension. From sunny California to wintry St. Petersburg reason lies in disrepute.

Despite the current "bad press" this book is a defense of reason and of a rational approach to life and living. It is not a defense of the naivety and dogmatism which passed for reason, and which were, in reality, the opposite to what is truly rational. It is an attempt to articulate a more authentic rational vision than the stereotypic Enlightenment message of the eighteenth and nineteenth centuries, a more authentic one than the "straw-man", which the contemporary anti-rationalists regularly attack.

This "new" approach begins with a clear concept of what reason is. It does not accept the distortions or limited perception of its enemies.

Reason is *not* logic. Conventional logic is a deductive system of thinking. It moves from premises to conclusions, using the conventional meanings of words to guide its procedures. If I say that all planets are round and that the earth is a planet, then I may logically conclude that the earth is round. If the premises are true, then the conclusion is true. But if the premises are false, the conclusion is false. Logic is willing to cooperate with both reality and fantasy.

If I say "that all planets are made out of green cheese" and that the earth is a planet, then I may logically conclude that the earth is made out of green cheese. Absurd premises yield absurd conclusions. Some of the craziest people in the world are logical. There are armies of paranoiacs, schizophrenics, visionaries and even theologians who are supremely logical. But they are also supremely irrational.

Reason is *not* cold. Being cold is just as emotional as being hot. There are cold emotions as well as hot emotions. If we are alive, we are expressing some kind of emotion or another. Cold indifference is as much a feeling as hot anger. Sometimes being "hot" may be more appropriate than being "cold." But it is not more emotional. It is impossible to respond to any situation without feeling.

Reason begins with a hot emotion, the desire to survive. It evolved as a tool for survival. The expanding neocortex of the brain was a positive mutation, enabling human beings to establish greater and greater control over their environments. Reason is a problem solver, focusing in on realistic causes and effects and realistic options. Most problems are attached to hot emotions. Reason is their faithful assistant. Rational physicians are not uncaring. Nor are rational engineers indifferent to the effects their work will have on the people they serve. Poets can be cold and detached, emotionally caught up in ethereal realms and unconcerned with the earthly agonies of ordinary people.

David Hume, a Scottish philosopher of the eighteenth century, put it well when he said; "We speak not strictly and philosophically when we talk of the combat of passion and of reason. Reason is, and ought only to be, the slave of the passions, and can never pretend to any other office than to serve and obey them." (*A Treatise of Human Nature*)

But reason is cautious. It needs to be wary of the vested interest of the emotions. Love generally sees only the virtues of the beloved and hate only the vices of the hated. The emotions are the fuel that energize us to respond to reality. But they cannot "create" the reality they want without harming our ability to deal effectively with the reality that is. If my parental love tells me that my children are failing in school because they are blameless geniuses with wicked teachers, I may not be able to help them. My emotions will not let me face the truth, and I cannot assist them so long as I persist in my fantasy.

Reason needs emotion as the motivation for being reasonable, as the driving force for trying to find out the truth in the first place. But it does not need emotion, whether hot or cold, to tell it what the truth is. If it throws aside all caution, it will become the prisoner of desire, a useless guide in a world of make believe, protecting us from the reality we do not want to face. The silly premises of our fantasy will yield equally silly conclusions.

Reason is first and above all, the willingness to face the facts, whether those facts are pleasant or unpleasant, whether those facts conform to the world we want or not. Facts are events in the real world. They have no agenda. They have no vested interests. They are simply there waiting to be discovered.

Reason begins with feeling, the "hot" need to solve the problems of daily living. It continues with observation, the testimony of our senses. It moves on to a vision of reality which we call the "hypothesis," a maybe statement about what the world is really like. The hypothesis needs a plan of action, a search for the evidence which will prove it true. We must be very careful not to let our vested interests intrude, especially if the hypothesis is something we want to be true or do not want to be true. In the end, we accept the verdict of the search. If the hypothesis turns into a truth, we will use it to guide our lives. If there is insufficient evidence, we will live with uncertainty. If there is no evidence, we will adjust our vision of reality, always aware that some delicious piece of new evidence will force us to reconsider tomorrow what we have decided today.

To be rational is to be realistic. To be realistic is to be sane. But it is not easy to be sane, especially in a world where reality and human desire are so far apart.

COURAGE

This book is also about the importance of courage.

The world that reason points to is often very harsh. Living in the real world is rarely blissful. It features daily frustration of desire and disappointment. Anxiety, stress and painful surprises are regular occurences. Indifference, rudeness and broken promises are part of the human landscape. Facing the trials of ordinary living requires extraordinary strength and courage.

We humans are prisoners of our imaginations. We can remember the past. We can worry about the future. We know that we are going to die. We are aware of dangers that we can neither see nor hear. The contented animal bliss of living in the *now* is not really possible, even when we pretend that it is. If most humans choose large doses of fantasy to alleviate the fear, that choice is understandable, even if it is not admirable.

Is it possible to live with the world that reason tells us exists? Is it possible to find happiness in a system of shrinking fantasies? Is it possible to look the real universe in its realistic face and discover that it is still wonderful and exciting?

There is no doubt about it. Realistic living takes courage. Our limitations are real. The immutable past is real. Aging is real. Death is real. Facing up to these realities, accepting them and designing our lives around them is no easy task. It is frightening. Only bravery can provide the bridge between desire and satisfaction.

There are many people who refuse to choose realism because courage is too demanding and too exhausting. They prefer the fantasy world where love and security are ultimately guaranteed. They conjure up a new universe to dispel their fears and resist any attempt to discover that it is an illusion. They believe because they need to believe. And many realists envy their seeming peace of mind.

The real world can allow us the opportunity of happiness. But it can also make us nervous. There are no guarantees. There is so much risk. There are so many choices. And the consequences are so uncertain.

Reason, by itself, is never enough. It can only point to the truth. It cannot give us the will to live with it. Reason needs courage to provide the fuel for happiness. Courage needs reason to chart the path.

This book is about the path of courage. This path requires knowledge, desire, will and persistence. To traverse it successfully is to find a new kind of strength. That strength is the strength of human dignity.

Over the last forty years, as a rabbi and as a founding leader in the movement of Humanistic Judaism, I have encountered many people who have taken this path of rational courage. Some failed along the way. Others inspired me with their bravery. The story of their determination and my own personal experience is contained in the message that follows.

PART ONE

A CRAZY WORLD

I

THE HUMAN CONDITION

WE LIVE IN A CRAZY WORLD. AT least, the world seems crazy.

What would the world be like if it were not crazy?

A non-crazy world would be a meaningful world. It would be a place of universal justice, in which all people would receive what they ultimately deserve. It would be a place of easy prediction where the consequences of our actions would be clearly seen. It would be a world of satisfaction, in which what we want is clearly achievable. It would be a good world, in which everything that happens to us, even the most painful, happens for the best.

A meaningful world is what we want. But it is also a world which we usually do not experience.

Harold does not believe that this is a world in which you get what you deserve. He is 35 years old and has just discovered he has bone cancer. He was abandoned as a child by his parents and was adopted by two childless, middle-aged people who were incapable of expressing any love. Despite these adversities he excelled in school and won a scholarship to a prestigious Eastern college. To earn sufficient money to supplement his scholarship money and to help support his aging parents, he held two part-time jobs. He found neither the time nor the money to provide for any minimum pleasure. He was driven by the ambition to succeed and the desire to receive the approval of his non-responsive parents and the admiration of his peers. Having graduated as one of the top students in his engineering class, he took a job with a leading automobile company in the Detroit area. His talent and zeal were so apparent that he rose rapidly on the executive ladder, a wonder boy of success. Three weeks after he received the news of his promotion to a junior vice-presidency and four weeks after his marriage to a woman he deeply loved, his physician sent him for further testing after a routine medical checkup. The verdict was a virulent bone cancer, the prelude to an early death. "I don't understand," he says over and over again.

Alice does not believe in a meaningful world. She is a school teacher. Both her mother and grandmother were school teachers. Her grandmother grew up on a farm and managed a one-room rural school house. Her mother was the principal of a leading high school. For Alice, getting a teaching certificate was not merely an opportunity for work; it was a commitment of love and an important family tradition. After graduation she found a job as a second-grade teacher. She adored her work. She had marvelous rapport with her students and their parents. But her principal posed a major problem. He was a charming, political appointee, a married man and a womanizer. He made advances to her. She resisted. She lost her job. Her union was weak and ineffective and unable to defend her interests. She is now unemployed. And the principal who tried to seduce her has now been promoted to manage a junior high school. Alice is bewildered. "Why did this happen to me? I didn't deserve it."

Harry does not believe that everything happens for the best in this world. He is the son of a Holocaust survivor who came to America after World War II. His mother was a native American who nursed Harry's father to health after a serious bout with tuberculosis. She waited twenty years for a child. When Harry arrived he became the center of her life. She worked hard to put Harry through college and watched with pride his winning a job in a prestigious New York accounting firm. Two years after her husband died, she suffered a major heart attack and could no longer work. Harry took care of her and brought her to live with him in New York. Five days after her arrival, Harry was mugged in a subway station while returning home late. His attackers, with no provocation, shot him in the back. He is now paralyzed from the neck down, an invalid for life. When the newspaper reporter suggested to him that he was lucky to be alive, he replied "With luck like that, you don't need a disaster." His mother, a deeply religious woman, kept saying "Why did God allow this to happen? He's such a good man."

Harold, Alice and Harry are only three people among millions who live lives of "injustice," who receive from the fates what they do not deserve. A crazy world is a universal experience. We all know innocent people who suffer. We all know rotten people who prosper. We can all testify to unwelcome and undeserved surprises, not only in the lives of friends and neighbors, but in our own lives as well.

So much of our daily experience in this modern, urban world testifies to its craziness. So much of our work, effort and devotion seem so futile. We train for professions that turn out to be obsolete. We invest ourselves in marriage partners who betray us. We give our love and nurturing to children who abandon us. We extend our devotion to friends who are never there when we need them. We work and save for the future, only to discover that we are too sick and too feeble to enjoy it. Some of the nicest people in our lives have such a hard time of it. And some of the meanest people sail through life with ease.

"Why me?" "Why them?" are universal questions we ask all the time. Most of us do not suffer the indignities that the Biblical Job endured. But we cannot help but ask his question-

"Why do the wicked live on, prosper and grow wealthy?
Their children are with them always . . .
Their homes are secure and without fear . . .
For the evil man is spared on the day of calamity."
                                                    (Job 21:7,8,9,30)

NO MORAL ORDER

A crazy world is a world without a moral order. A moral order is different from a physical order. Laws of nature are part of the physical order. But the laws of nature have no moral agenda. The law of gravity is as willing to cooperate with good people as with bad people. It will allow food supplies to be dropped on needy refugees. It will, just as easily, permit evil men to throw innocent victims off of parapets.

A meaningful world is more than an orderly world. The universe of modern science is an orderly universe. But its order grinds on with no apparent concern for the victims of its relentless march. Earthquakes rumble, volcanos erupt, floods pour over their river banks, all of them sweeping their human debris into the path of their destruction. This recurring holocaust is the result of a natural order which has natural and irresistible causes with natural, irresistible and inevitable consequences. But it lacks the kind of order that gives the universe meaning.

Sadists are orderly. But a sadistic universe is not the kind of world we want to live in. We want to live in a world governed by moral law, a world in which everything that happens happens for the good. We want to live in a universe in which the powers that govern and control our destiny are neither malicious nor cruel. Simply knowing that they are orderly is little comfort at all.

Geologists can demonstrate that the eruption of Pinatubo in the Philippines was inevitable and unavoidable. But what comfort is that to the young mother of four children who lost them all in the deadly ash. Meteorologists can explain why the expansion of the Sahara is the natural consequence of predictable climatic change. But what consolation is that to a hardworking farmer and family man who has lost his only means of substance because of the drought? Traffic controllers can estimate that there will be a certain percentage of fatal airplane crashes during a given year. But what kind of answer is that to a grieving mother who has lost her only child in a freak air disaster? *Kismet* only works if Allah has some good moral reason for doing to you what he does.

Understanding why something terrible happens does not make what happens morally more tolerable. Knowing that Hitler was an abused child and that abused children can turn into murderers does not make the Holocaust less horrible. Becoming aware that criminally assaultive males may suffer from some malformation of the genes does not make their crimes against innocent victims morally more acceptable. Excusing them does not excuse the universe. A just universe would not allow such things to happen. It either would never have arranged to produce such aggressors, or it would have arranged to separate them from their victims. From a moral perspective, the order of the universe can definitely be improved.

As long as we experience the world as unfair, and most of us do at sometime or other, we also experience the world as "crazy."

CRUELTY

A crazy world is a world that "teases." It fills us with very intense desires and never allows us to fully satisfy them.

The strongest human desire is the desire to live. The struggle for survival, whether our own personal one or that of the people we love, is often relentless and sometimes bitter. Around every corner we are confronted by the eternal enemy, the specter of death. There is a fundamental cruelty in a universe that fills us with the passion for life and simultaneously endows us with the inevitability of dying. Contrary to the cliches, death does not become easier and less frightening with age. It is often more painful because we are filled with regret for all that we failed to do and for all that we failed to see. When there is no longer any hope of recouping our losses, expiring is no great comfort. Certainly, desiring death as an alternative to excruciating pain or to humiliating feebleness is little consolation. The universe could have arranged for no death at all or for dying to be easier.

There are so many things we want to do and experience. And there is never enough time to satisfy our desires. By the time we understand our mistakes it is often too late to correct them. By the time we are wise enough to appreciate the good things in life, we are too old to take advantage of them. By the time we discover who we really are, we begin to fall apart. It is true that youth is wasted on the young. But that truth precisely dramatizes the cruelty of the world. Reality does not fit our desires. Death mocks our passions.

Ben is a middle-aged physician who has established a successful but not exciting practice as a dermatologist. When he was young, he desired to be a concert pianist. He possessed extraordinary musical abilities, but had never been able to develop his talents fully. When he graduated from high school, he won a scholarship to the Eastman School in Rochester, N.Y. But his parents felt that a musical career was financially *iffy* and insisted that he enter the pre-med program of the local university. He surrendered to their demands, finished medical school, married a doctor's daughter and fathered four children, none of whom turned out to be very talented, very loving or very interesting. He is very disappointed with his life; but he does not see much opportunity for change. It is too late to become a concert pianist. And his sense of responsibility to his wife and his children's education prevents any sudden reversal of life style. He feels trapped and resentful. His "mid-life crisis" may be typical. But it is unique to him and very painful. Aging, dying and death are too close to give him another chance. He keeps saying over and over again "If only I *hadn't* listened to my parents . . ." He often remarks, "Why do we come to understand what is most important in our life when it is too late to do anything about it?"

Elizabeth is an accomplished journalist. She is an attractive woman 45 years old, lively, open and frank. She was an early militant feminist determined never to repeat the mistakes her mother made. When she was an undergraduate in college she resolved never to marry and never to have children. The intensity of her zeal filled her with a kind of euphoria for many years. She pursued her career in journalism and avoided thinking about alternatives. She even had contempt for many of her friends who had chosen to be early mothers and housewives. When she was 40 she met a man five years her junior who literally swept her off her feet. Although a little embarrassed after her militant rhetoric for so many years, she married him. Her life changed. The desire for a child entered her consciousness in a very powerful way. She wanted very much to be a mother. She wanted to give birth to her own child. But she was unable to conceive. She went from doctor to doctor, clinic to clinic. She even traveled to fertility centers in London and Melbourne. To no avail. The physicians told her that her body was changing and that she was too old to bear children. The news depressed her for a while. Her husband was opposed to adoption. She felt cheated. "It's a crazy world," she said. "We find out what we want when we can no longer have it."

A crazy world is a world where desire is too strong, time is too short, aging is too relentless and death is too eager. Sometimes the universe appears to be a bad joke.

DISAPPOINTMENT

A crazy world is a world where the best laid plans come to naught, where the finest of our labors turns out to be disappointingly different from what we imagined it would be. After all, the good life is anticipation, looking forward to good things. We love surprises, especially when they relieve the routine of daily living. But we do not love surprises when they shatter dreams and hopes, when they turn the fragile order of our existence into chaos.

What we want most out of life is to have a sense of control over what happens to us. We want to feel that the world we live in is not chaotic, that the future is predictable, that there are certain guarantees which support our right to happiness. No feeling is worse than feeling totally out of control, the victim of the passing whims of the world. Pursuing success is too hard to have it summarily dismissed by a careless universe. So much of our early childhood is devoted to convincing us that effort and determination are worthwhile, that they produce positive results, that they are justified by the success they bring.

But the world we live in is far less predictable than we would want it to be. On the grand, cosmic, non-human scale, it is eminently predictable. Mathematics, physics and astronomy have made the movements of the sun, moon and the stars a dance of unerring scientific prophecy. But on the small, earthly, human scale of daily living, existence is far more uncertain. History, political science, economics and sociology are far less scientific than they pretend to be. Unlike the stars, human behavior has to be viewed in all its grubby detail, with all the chaos that conscious and unconscious minds bring to any situation. On the level of daily living, we are not flying over the forest. We are living in the middle of the trees. On the microcosmic level, which may be just as important as the cosmic one, events seem much more chaotic. Life seems much more uncertain.

Gloria understands that uncertainty. She planned her life so well, at least she thought she had. She was determined to find a husband, devote herself to him and their children and reap the benefits of a loving supportive family. She met Al when she was in high school. They dated for eight years, until he graduated from the university. Before he entered graduate school, they married. While Al was devoted full time to pursuing his doctorate in physics, she worked full time to pay for his education and to take care of their growing family, three children in four years. Through all this trying period, Al was a marvelous friend to Gloria. Despite the strains of study, Al always found time to make Gloria feel special and loved. Friends commented on how perfectly matched they were. Even after Al received his doctorate and a teaching job at a prestigious university, the bond between them never seemed to diminish or grow routine. Gloria was very happy, very content with her life. She believed that the investment of time, energy and loyalty that she had made were justified by the success of her life. Then one day her security was shattered. Al arrived home late distraught and somewhat incoherent. He told her he wanted a divorce. He told her that he was in love with one of his graduate students, that he wanted to marry her, that the romance happened very suddenly, that he was sorry and felt very guilty. But he wanted to leave this relationship of twenty-two years. Gloria was stunned. Her present distress comes from more than the rejection, more than the loss of somebody she loved, more than the prospect of living alone and having to deal with the needs of three traumatized children, more than the resentment, anger and betrayal that she feels. It comes also from her sense of losing control of her life, her almost non-comprehending bewilderment that everything she has counted on to provide security, structure and meaning to her life is disappearing. She says that she feels she is going crazy.

Losing control may make us feel crazy. It can also make us feel that the world is crazy. Unexpected surprises undermine our sense of security and order. Indeed, the universe may be governed by laws that determine every event that happens, even the smallest and most insignificant event. Indeed, some complex underlying order may account for the trauma we are presently experiencing. But that order is not something we can feel. All we know is that the order which we sought to bring to our lives has collapsed, and the world seems chaotic and crazy. We have lost control of our lives. And for us that is disorder.

Dr. Pangloss in Voltaire's Candide, echoing the German philosopher Leibniz, maintained that this world was the best of all possible worlds. Even the Lisbon earthquake could not shake his faith. For him the human condition was a just condition and this universe a just universe.

But what if we cannot believe that? What if we experience the world as not the best of all possible worlds? What if we experience the universe as a slightly or extravagantly "crazy" place?

How do we cope?

2

THE COMFORTS OF TRADITION

RELIGION HAS BEEN THE MOST popular way of coping with a crazy world. From the very beginnings of history traumatized men and women have sought to compensate for the absurdities of the natural world with the comforts of the supernatural. If death was not real, if this life was followed by the rewards and punishments of the afterlife, then the universe would take on a meaning that ordinary human experience had not found.

People disagree on the origins of religion. For pious believers, religion was created by the gods or God himself. The Deity communicated through divinely chosen prophets what the nature of the universe really was and what he expected human beings to do. The

God of Judaism spoke through Moses. The God of Christianity spoke through Christ. The God of Islam gave his message through Mohammed. Religion is a divine invention, which is superior to any human invention because it is divine. Divinity has access to power and wisdom which human beings can never reach.

For liberal believers and for non-believers religion is a human creation. It is a human response to a crazy world. It is a human attempt to deal with the hopelessness and helplessness that so many people experience in their daily lives. It is a human denial of what makes life meaningless and intolerable. If death is cruel and unfair, then death is not real. If human power is too limited to achieve happiness and fulfillment, then another greater power is available if only we know how to tap into it. God and the gods are the way human beings conceive of this power.

Personal gods do not have mysterious origins. They look like the strong parents and strong leaders we so much depend on, parents and leaders who die and leave us alone. If we do not wish to be abandoned we come to believe that they exist elsewhere, in a supernatural and divine form. They continue to rule our lives and to help us. They continue to make demands on us and to judge our behavior. And because they are like our parents and our leaders, only stronger and wiser, they receive from us the respect and reverence we give to the authorities which shape our lives. If we both fear and love them, we do so because we both feared and loved our parents. If we both obey and appease them, we do so because we obeyed and appeased the fathers and mothers of our childhood. For pious believers, parents and leaders are the reflection of the gods. For critical believers, the gods are the reflection of parents and leaders.

Primary religion rests on four foundations. It rests, first of all, on the belief in supernatural power. Supernatural power is different from natural power because it is limitless, because it is not confined by the laws of nature. It is a continuously renewable energy that is never exhausted. It is a miracle force that never has to pay attention to the normal boundaries of space and time. If it is controllable and manageable, then it ends up in the world of magic. If it resists control and human management then it enters the realm of religion. In the world of religion human beings have access to this power but they are never able to subdue it or to manipulate it. Like electricity, supernatural energy has the ability to help us and also to harm us with its intensity. Unlike electricity, it cannot be measured or reduced to servitude.

Personal religion also rests on the belief in the spiritual world. The spiritual world is the supernatural world of supernatural spirits. Supernatural spirits are beings that possess supernatural power. They may be gods or goddesses. They may be angels or demons. They may be ghosts or eternal souls of the dead. They may be loving or cruel. They may be friendly or hostile. But they are all united by their possession of power. If they were not powerful, they would not be interesting. Human beings have not been attracted to the spiritual world because it is spiritual. They have been attracted to it because it is powerful.

For most of human history people have believed that they lived in a double world of natural powers and supernatural powers, of ordinary beings and extraordinary spirits. Peasants and kings imagined that they were surrounded by invisible forces that could rescue them or destroy them. These forces could not be ignored, in the same way that one could not ignore the sun and the wind. In fact, the sun and the wind might derive their own energy from their supernatural connection. The spiritual world needed to be confronted and dealt with. One had to learn how to avoid its harm and to win its benefits. Paying no attention to it was the road to disaster. It was worse than ignoring the weather or disobeying parents.

Worship is the way in which religious people in all cultures have dealt with the supernatural and spiritual. Since the invisible forces cannot always be magically manipulated, and since they possess extraordinary awareness and penetrating consciousness, they need to be appeased. Even if they are loving, they need to be appeased, because, like loving parents, they expect respect and recognition. The most familiar form of appeasement and devotion is the bringing of gifts. Gifts to the gods are called sacrifices. Some gifts were food. Others were gold and silver. Still others were words of praise and adoration. In time, the rituals of sacrifice were turned over to experts to make sure that no mistakes were made in the presence of the demanding gods. These experts became the priests and ministers of the divinities. Elaborate places of sacrifice called temples emerged. Elaborate symbols of the spiritual world evolved in the form of statues and vestments. In the end, the gods looked very much like exaggerated forms of the kings, chiefs and parents who were the visible rulers of the natural world.

An alternative to sacrifice and prayer was mystical devotion. This option was confined to a small number of people. The purpose of mystical devotion was the direct experience of the supernatural and spiritual. The psychics of the ancient world were called prophets, or holy men, and achieved their direct contact with the gods through ecstatic trances, meditation, discipline, self-hypnosis and drugs. Mystical experiences were often supremely thrilling because they were direct contacts with the power of the supernatural. But they were also dangerous, because brushing up against the spiritual could also burn as well as heal. Many established religions came to frown on mystical experiments, fearing they might lead to personal revelations that contradicted traditional teachings. Mystics rarely ended up in the center of the religious hierarchy. They moved around the periphery, challenging faith through direct intuition.

As religion developed, it went beyond its primary functions. It attached to itself a whole host of secondary roles that were not intrinsically religious. Religion was married to ethics. Standards of right and wrong, which had evolved over long periods of time in the secular world of problem solving, were turned into the commands of the gods. Morality received supernatural authority to justify it and supernatural power to enforce it. What had formerly been common sense and folk custom became the voice of God. The traditional ethics of each culture became divine. Divinity spoke with as many voices as there were cultures.

There is no fundamental reason why religion and morality have to be united. The moral authority of the gods does not lie in the fact that they are gods. It lies in the fact that we believe that they are good. Knowing that they are good must come from some source other than religious. Supernatural and spiritual power can be used for evil purposes. Demons and devils are as much a part of the religious world as angels and saints. Turning God into the arbiter of morals may be customary. But it is not essential.

Secondary religion is expressed in the intimate connection of religion and patriotism. Many people cannot distinguish between their ethnic loyalties and their religious commitments. Religions often evolve in the struggle of ethnic groups to achieve power and success. The Muslim conquest of Western Asia cannot be separated from the Arab conquest of the same world. The Greek resistance to Arab imperialism cannot easily be separated from the Greek Orthodox resistance to the same power. Ethnic pride and religious fervor often go hand in hand. Trying to be Polish without being Catholic is not easy. Trying to be Indian without being Hindu is a hard task. Many people practice the religions of their parents as much for ethnic reasons as for religious ones. Abandoning their religion is the same as abandoning their ancestors.

One of the reasons why religious fundamentalism is sweeping so much of the Third World is that it is completely tied up with nationalism. With no history of secular culture many Asian and African nations express their hostility to the West through religious fervor. Patriots cannot distinguish between their love of God and their loyalty to their nation. "God, King and Country" is a universal cry. But there is no fundamental reason why religion and nationalism have to be married. It just happened that way.

Both ethics and patriotism expanded the power and scope of religion. Religious institutions went beyond temples and shrines. They included schools and hospitals and national monuments. In time, almost every aspect of the daily life of the average peasant or lord was governed by religious authority. Education and welfare started with religion. But they are not intrinsic to religion. They can just as easily be arranged by secular specialists, whether public or private. The connection is historical rather than essential.

Basic traditional religion, religion in its primary form, is one of the most compelling human institutions ever developed. Its significance does not only lie in its connection to these historical functions. Its significance lies in the fact that, for most of the people of the world, it keeps the world from becoming "crazy."

Traditional religion, if its claims are true, gives us access to an extraordinary power. With this power, life does not have to be a cruel frustration. Life does not have to be wanting what we cannot have. With supernatural power, happiness is a real possibility, whether happiness happens here on earth or somewhere else. Salvation is not a dream that teases us with its inaccessibility. It is a destination awaiting our arrival if only we know what to do.

Traditional religion makes the world a meaningful world. In its monotheistic form, God is a supreme being, just and loving, who has created the universe according to his divine plan. Nothing happens in this universe which is not for the good. Nothing happens which, in the end, is unjust. With our limited human perspective, we may imagine that what is really good is evil. We may imagine that pain and suffering are tragic and bad. But, at the final count, the wicked will be punished. The righteous will be rewarded. Everything will be in its moral place.

Traditional religion drives away all the unpleasant emotions that a meaningless world provokes. It rescues us from despair with the promise of eternal life. It relieves our loneliness with the presence of a divine friend. It dismisses our anger with a deep and abiding acceptance of whatever happens to us. It conquers our fear with the awesome energy of supernatural power. It washes away our disillusionment with the message of therapeutic suffering. It keeps us from feeling forlorn with the experience of a just and moral order.

There are many religious ways to make the world meaningful. The history of religion features many varieties of supernatural power, many scenarios of supernatural action. Some religions have lasted for only a short time. Others have endured for hundred of years. Some have been confined to one nation and a small territory. Others have won the allegiance of many nations and whole continents. The key to survival and success is more than the political, economic and social institutions which come to support religion. The key is the power of the message, the degree to which the revelation drives away the "craziness" of the universe.

Five well-known traditional religious systems testify to this truth: Judaism, Christianity, Islam, Hinduism and Buddhism.

Judaism, in its original form, was mildly successful. It was the Judaism of the Torah, centered around the rewards and punishments of this life. Obedience to God guaranteed happiness here on earth. The righteous man would discover that his crops would grow, his children would prosper and his enemies would be vanquished. But human experience contradicted this promise. And the priests of Jerusalem had only a dismal afterlife in a dismal place called Sheol to offer as an alternative. It was the coming of the Pharisees, led by the rabbis, that changed the fortunes of Judaism. With the Pharisees and the rabbis came the belief in the resurrection of the dead. In the end of days God would arrange for a final judgment. He would raise the dead from their graves, judge the living and the dead, and assign the defendants to either the heaven of the Garden of Eden or the hell of Gehenna. With the promise of a glorious afterlife for the righteous, Judaism became a popular religion. In the cities of the Greek and Roman empires thousands of non-Jews converted to Judaism. If it were not for the painful, and, for some, humiliating requirement of circumcision, thousands more would have joined. The rabbis proclaimed a God that was strong enough and just enough to make everything right in the end. And the ancient world responded with enthusiasm.

Christianity built on the message of Pharisaic Judaism, rescued it from circumcision and ethnic parochialism, and added the compelling story of a suffering and triumphant God. The Church explained human suffering and gave it meaning. If we suffer it is because we are sinful. And if we die, it is because we deserve it. But, in the end, the grace of a compassionate God who, like us, has endured the pain of human degradation, will rescue us and make it possible for us to attain the happiness and salvation we so deeply yearn for. We will rise to a glorious eternal life in the very same way that he did. The key to salvation is neither wealth, status nor power. It is the simple faith that God will do what he promises to do. Even women and slaves will be the equal of the mighty in the Kingdom of God. In the world of the Greeks and the Romans there were few messages that could defeat the pessimism and confusion of the suffering masses. Christianity did. And it became the most successful religious system the world has ever seen.

Islam mirrored the messages of Judaism and Christianity. Mohammed proclaimed the power and justice of Allah. To recognize his power and dominion, to worship Him, to obey His laws, is to obtain entry to Paradise and to eternal happiness. All is determined by the might of Allah yet free will is given. If one freely chooses to surrender himself to the will of Allah, then that surrender justifies eternal rewards. The success of Islam lay not only in the intimidating might of conquering Arab armies. It lay also in the irresistible promise of forever and ever bliss. The world of the Prophet, despite all its frightening travail, was a meaningful world. Justice prevailed in the end. Happiness was the reward of virtue.

Hinduism evolved in a setting independent of the cultural and political history of the West. Its beginnings lie in both the former religion of the dark Dravidian aborigines of the Indian sub-continent and in the warrior religion of the white Aryan invaders. Its form was shaped by Aryan Brahmin priests who controlled the worship of the gods and who encouraged the racism of the caste system. Power, status and wealth were distributed in accordance with birth and ethnic origin. In time a doctrine arose to justify this social development. It was the principle of *karma*, which maintained that every action had a moral consequence, and that pain and suffering were the result of evil deeds. But what evil deeds?

What evil deeds had innocent children or dark-skinned saints committed? The answer was clear. The human soul was immortal. It moved from body to body, from lifetime to lifetime. The good deeds and the bad deeds of one life were rewarded and punished in the next. The wicked Brahmin of this incarnation would become the humiliated outcast of the next embodiment. Even though we could not remember past lives or envision future ones, the relentless morality of *karma* and reincarnation prevailed. The world, with all its anguish and despair, was a just and meaningful world. Unlike the message of Western religion, which only spoke of future immortality, the message of Hinduism proclaimed past immortality as well. The pain of today was not a test of faith. It was a justified punishment for an unjustified action. The wheel of justice turns and we are all attached to it.

Buddhism was an offshoot of Hinduism in the same way that Christianity was the child of Judaism. It broke away from its mother religion by rejecting both the Brahmin priesthood and the caste system. But it retained the belief in reincarnation and the wheel of justice. It also went beyond the karma notion that suffering was the punishment for evil action. It emphasized the doctrine that suffering was the consequence of desire. When we want something we suffer the anguish of not having it. If we wanted nothing, there would be no anguish. Despair, disappointment, frustration and anxiety would vanish from our lives. If only we could train ourselves to desire nothing, then we would transcend all suffering, even the wheel of justice, and enter peaceful oblivion. Aristocratic Buddhism devoted much time to this escape from desire. But popular Buddhism found comfort in the world of karma and reincarnation. Being born in a better heaven seemed good enough. And the saints who helped us get there deserved our worship and adoration. With no caste system and with this reassuring vision of a meaningful world, Buddhism won the heart of eastern Asia.

Now, Judaism, Christianity, Islam, Hinduism and Buddhism are different religions. There are many disagreements among them about faith, ritual and spirituality. There have been violent disputes over the nature of God, his names and his power. There have emerged different prophets, different revelations and different scriptures. Even the cultural contexts in which they arose provide sharp contrasts. But they are all united by a general agreement that transcends all their differences and unites them in a common message.

This message is more than agreement about the existence of spiritual powers and supernatural worlds. It is the clear affirmation that we do *not* live in a crazy world. Justice, whether in the form of a personal God or impersonal karma, rules the universe. It is relentless and inescapable. Whether one is a pious Jew, Christian, Muslim, Hindu or Buddhist, good deeds are revealed and wicked deeds are punished. The world has a moral order. The world is meaningful. The success of successful religions surely lies in a belief in a powerful God. But it especially lies in a belief in a *just* God.

In its most extreme form the message denies the very reality of evil. The ancient Boethius, a Christian philosopher in later Roman times maintained: "There is nothing that an omnipotent God could not do . . . Then can God do evil? No. So that evil is nothing, since that is what he cannot do who can do anything." (*The Consolation of Philosophy*)

DECLINE OF RELIGION

The power of religion is undeniable. For untold centuries it controlled the world view of all people all over the world. It explained their suffering. It gave them hope. It justified their acceptance of whatever the fates dished out to them. Without this belief system the power of priests and ritual would not exist. A crazy world is not easy for most people to take. They will do almost anything to avoid it.

But, in modern times, the power of religion has declined. New ideas and new forces have moved into the forefront. They have also challenged not only the power of religious institutions. They have challenged the very ideas which made these institutions powerful.

These new ideas and new forces were not initially hostile to religion. They were even embraced by people who were very religious and who wished to improve the quality of their lives. Nobody fully understood the changes that were taking place. But they were very profound. In the end many people could no longer accept the old answers to the question of meaning.

What were these profound changes?

The revolution is summarized by two words, *science* and *capitalism.*

The age of science is the knowledge revolution of the last four centuries. This revolution was characterized by four traumatic innovations. The first was a new method for the discovery of truth which challenged ancestral tradition and folk wisdom by an appeal to experimentation and evidence. The second was the overthrow of the basic beliefs that most people cherished concerning the origins and nature of the universe, life and people. The third was the never-ending surge of new information and knowledge about the world, which was too relentless and too complex for any single individual to master. And the fourth was the conceiving and producing of new technologies which gave to human beings the power that formerly belonged only to the gods.

The age of science shook the age of religion to its foundations.

The universe of the Bible was no longer believable. Priests, ministers and rabbis were no longer the only or the best spokesmen of truth. Wisdom was no longer eternal and unchangeable. The aura of power and salvation floated from the body of religion to the new body of reason.

The age of capitalism went hand in hand with the age of science. Each enabled the other to be successful. Capitalism was more than an economic revolution. It was a social revolution that radically transformed human relations and human expectations. It too was expressed in four traumatic innovations. The first was the acknowledgement that trade, business and manufacturing were just as respectable as farming and fighting. The second was the emergence of a new ambitious middle class of urbanites and professionals who were no longer willing to accept suffering as the norm of human existence. The third was the massive movement of millions of people from the countryside to the new centers of urban life. And the fourth was the powerful belief, implicit in the enthusiastic embrace of the new technology, that progress and salvation were possible here on earth.

Science and capitalism radically changed the world of religion. They shifted the focus of human attention from the afterlife to this life. They raised the level of human expectations. They elevated reason as a competitor to faith. They promoted toleration in an urban society where people of different cultures were forced to live side by side. They made men and women more aware of their own natural power to change and control their environment.

They also profoundly affected the way people dealt with the "meaningful universe" of tradition. It was hard for many people to still believe that God was concerned with the human moral agenda. When the earth was seen as the center of the universe, God's concern was believable. But when the earth turned out to be an astronomical speck revolving around an insignificant star in one galaxy among trillions, that concern seemed much less plausible.

It was hard for many people to still believe that the laws of nature were instruments of divine justice and that the God who invented them would suspend them in order to perform miracles of compassion. Maybe, if there was a God, He simply created the universe, set it in motion and let the laws of nature take it from there.

It was hard for many people to still believe in a supernatural world filled with immortal souls and spirits on their way to reincarnation. The connection of the human mind to the human brain and nervous system was so dramatically demonstrated by evidence that the separation of the two became less and less believable. The evolution of the mind was attached to the evolution of the brain. Mental events were also material events. Organic events were variations on inorganic events.

It was hard for many people to still believe in the "meaningful universe" of the old religions. Ironically, as people felt themselves gaining more and more control over their own environment, they also felt themselves losing control over their own moral agenda. Things happened because they needed to happen. But they did not happen because they needed to be good.

The world of science and capitalism revealed an orderly but "crazy" universe. Everything happened for a reason. But not everything happened for the best. The euphoria of human power was matched by the despair that many felt in a universe devoid of divine moral guarantees.

3

THE SECULAR ALTERNATIVE

SECULARISM IS THE WORLD VIEW molded by science and capitalism. It stands in opposition to traditional religion. It seeks to answer the same questions that religion does. But it provides different answers. One of the basic questions it addresses is the central question of this book. Does life have any meaning? And, if it does, where does it come from?

When religion began to decline, secularism emerged to fill the emotional and intellectual vacuum that many felt. Negative secularists simply ceased to be religious, but never bothered to articulate an alternative philosophy of life for themselves. Positive secularists lost their old faith but were eager for a new one, a faith that burned with the same fervor as the one they had abandoned and could no longer believe in.

Secularism began with the importance of reason. It began with people solving problems by learning from experience and by testing the consequences of their behavior. Human civilization rests on the achievements of millions of anonymous people who enhanced human survival through their own ingenuity. They made stone weapons and hunted game. They planted seeds and reaped the harvest. They invented the wheel and made wagons. They found plant fibre and wove cloth for clothing. Although they never used the word "reason," they discovered the relationship between cause and effect. They also discovered how to reproduce causes and how to reproduce effects. Where what they were doing was not regarded as sacred, they were perfectly willing to modify their behavior on the basis of trial and error. Most of these ingenious people were religious. And they saw no conflict between their religion and solving problems by appealing to experience. Long before anybody used the word "rational," people were using reason.

But time produced a conflict. Knowledge that was acquired through trial and error turned into tradition. It became sacred, untouchable and unchangeable. It found its way into sacred scriptures where it was revered and worshiped as the absolute truth. Reason was replaced by faith. The pragmatic discovery of one age became the eternal wisdom of the next. Faith is trust. It is the trust we place in the reliability of our ancestors. Rational people use umbrellas because it protects them from the rain. Faithful people use umbrellas because their ancestors used umbrellas. Even when they move to the desert, even when it never rains, they will continue to use umbrellas, if using them is part of their sacred tradition.

Sacredness and holiness are religious concepts that are opposed to reason. Reason is always sensitive to consequences and effects. It assumes that human behavior ought to be related to human survival and human happiness. It assumes that when circumstances change, behavior should change to meet the circumstances. It cannot accept rituals and procedures that are fixed and unchangeable. Sacred laws and sacred acts are, by their very nature, unchangeable. They are frozen in time. In the world of the sacred, people have long since forgotten why their ancestors chose to do what they did. They do what they do out of obedience and respect. Tradition carries its own authority.

The power of the sacred is reinforced by institutions and books. Priests, temples and holy scriptures give it both a setting and support. If priesthoods become very powerful, the area of experimentation grows narrower and narrower. Piety replaces testing. Quotations from holy writ replace new hypothesis. Life derives its tempo from the rhythm of imitation. The flexibility of the secular becomes increasingly unfashionable.

Twice during the last ten thousand years the devotees of reason have conducted successful rebellions against sacred authority. The first was in Greece in the fifth and sixth centuries B.C. Teachers, called philosophers, established secular schools where their students would be taught in a secular way. Reason, not sacred tradition, was the criterion of truth. Even though many of the philosophers, including Plato and Aristotle, were dogmatic and less than rational, they pioneered a mode of inquiry, a method of justification, that still survives. Faith was not enough. Being traditional was not enough. Something more was required.

The philosophers, although they did not agree among themselves, were agreed that there was nothing too sacred to be questioned and challenged. In the end, one might embrace a traditional answer, but not for traditional reasons. Protagoras and Socrates, Zeno and Epicurus were philosophic opponents. Yet they stood together in their resistance to piety. They were the pioneers of a new way of dealing with the truth. They had become self-aware rationalists. And they would no longer be intimidated by the sacred.

The blossoming of Greek philosophy, a first in the annals of human history, was destroyed by the dogmatic power of a new successful religion. Born in Judea, Christianity appropriated the sacred tradition of the Jews and added the compelling story of the Messiah Jesus to flesh out its winning message. Having achieved supremacy in the Roman Empire, it demanded conformity of all Roman citizens. The philosophic schools of Athens and the Greek world were designated as enemies and infidels. They were closed down, their teachers dispersed and their books burned. The brief debut of secular thinking was followed by active repression and the punishment of secular heresies. Yet, even this age of intense religion could not forget the Greeks entirely. Priests and theologians felt compelled to justify their sacred doctrines by making appeals to Plato and Aristotle.

The second rebellion against sacred authority was the prelude to modern times. It was called the Enlightenment and boldly challenged the religious establishments. Beginning in the seventeenth century, the Enlightenment philosophers abandoned piety and proclaimed the supremacy of Reason. Descartes and Spinoza, Hobbes and Leibniz changed the rules of intellectual discourse. The dialogue was now secular. Appeals to the Bible and to Church doctrine were now unacceptable. Truth stood on the two pillars of intuition and evidence.

The Enlightenment rested on the foundation of the European Renaissance. Three centuries before the coming of the Enlightenment, the prosperous cities of Italy and the Netherlands fostered a revival of Greek and Roman learning. Greek literature, Greek mythology,

Greek sculpture and Greek architecture invaded the medieval world and became, in the hands of their admirers, the signs of high fashion. The people who supported this rebirth (renaissance) of Greek culture were the new masters of urban wealth, princes and bourgeois magnates, who needed a different vision of life from the one that the priests had been touting. The old Christian vision was too tied up with the feudal system and the warrior lords and former peasants that made it possible. Asceticism and opposition to profit-making were not the stuff out of which economic growth could be conjured. The new order needed a new approach to human powers and human ambitions. By the end of the sixteenth century, despite the intense wars generated by the Reformation, many people in Europe were ready for a secular revolution. Inspired by Greek culture, they were ready to assault the Church.

The proponents of the Enlightenment saw themselves as the enemies of superstition. Using the weapon of Reason they assaulted the intellectual fortresses of the religious establishment. They offered a new creed to the educated. Salvation belonged to this world and human power was sufficient to guarantee salvation. Nothing stood in the way of human advancement except human ignorance. Dismiss the darkness of human ignorance with the clear light of Reason and people would be free to find happiness here on earth.

The philosophers of the eighteenth century rejected the world of faith. With Voltaire they mocked the foolishness of religion. With Hume they made the supernatural disappear. With Kant they dismissed any attempt to prove the existence of God. The French Revolution completed their work. Divine-right monarchs were dethroned. Religion was separated from government. Education was turned over to secular bureaucrats.

The philosophers of the nineteenth century became even

bolder and more radical. With Bentham they turned ethics into the pursuit of happiness. With Mill they liberated the individual from community restraint and found the virtues of liberal democracy. With Darwin they dismissed heavenly man and made him the child of earth and nature.

A secular society emerged to replace the religious society of the past. Religion was still strong and significant. But it no longer controlled the centers of political and economic power. And it was possible to lead a secular life without any need of turning to the institutions of religion. Education, welfare and work were in secular hands.

But this triumphant secularism suffered an intrinsic weakness that the euphoria of victory could not completely hide. Without God and the afterlife, the troublesome question of meaning became a thorn in the secular side. If the only real world is the natural world and the natural world is filled with unfairness and injustice, then the universe is devoid of meaning. For the winners in this new drama of science and capitalism, the question was unimportant. But for the losers and malcontents it was of ultimate importance.

Secularism responded to this challenge by stealing a page from traditional religion. It took the notion of heaven and a Messianic utopia and transferred it to this world. It promised total salvation here on earth. A world of peace, harmony, love and plenty was not a supernatural experience. It was the inevitable outcome of all the social forces operating in history. The name of this social phenomenon was *progress*. Even if we, personally, do not live to experience utopia, our descendants and all of humanity will. In the end, things are getting better and better.

The doctrine of progress was essential to the success of the secularist message. It gave meaning to the universe. It guaranteed utopia without God. Many variations on this basic theme emerged.

Liberals, like Mill, saw personal freedom as the chief vehicle for progress. Socialists, like Proudhon, found equality to be the trigger. Nationalists, like Hegel, discovered the key in state power. Vitalists, like Shaw and Bergson, believed that the source of progress lay in the upward striving of superior individuals. Marxists claimed the leading role for the revolution.

At the very beginning the notion of progress was easy to sustain. The dramatic rise in the standard of living of most people in the Western world generated hope. And the advance of technology, made people feel confident about their future. Secular utopias were as believable as the sacred heavens of the past.

In fact, the vision of secular utopias, replaced the religious vision for most people. Whether capitalist or communist, the future was going to be wonderful.

There was no reason to be forlorn. Human effort and human striving would be vindicated in the human happiness that would follow. Life had meaning because the world had meaning. Secularism, ironically, took on the passions of a religion. And much of the secularist message was an echo of the old established faith.

The marriage of religion and secularism produced liberal religion. The symbols and vocabulary of traditional Christianity and Judaism were preserved. But a new secular message was substituted for the old religious one. By the beginning of the twentieth century the new secular religion had taken over the Protestant establishment in North America. By the end of the century it had captured the Catholic Church. Along the way it won the allegiance of most Western Jews.

Liberal religion rested on three foundations. The first was a naturalistic theology. The old God of reward and punishment was pushed aside. He was much too anthropomorphic and intrusive for secular credibility. He was replaced by three alternatives. There was the deistic God who invented the world and then allowed it to run all by itself. There was the pantheistic God who was one and the same with nature. And there was the "symbolic" God, a hodge-podge of forces and powers in the world that supported human welfare. Newton preferred the first. Spinoza preferred the second and John Dewey chose the third.

The second foundation was religious psychology. In traditional religion devotees spoke of God and the spirit world as realities out there. In liberal religion God and spirituality became internal events. Religion was turned into the religious experience. Theology became a department of psychology. The important thing was not the objective existence of God (which, after all, could no longer be demonstrated). It was the subjective experience of the spiritual, the sacred, the holy. Whether the experience corresponded to some reality out there was no longer significant. If the experience enriched your life, that reality was sufficient to justify its indulgence. Religion was important because it was good for us, because it made us feel good, because we needed God. Every person's religious experience was subjective and personal. You could not evaluate mine. I could not evaluate yours. All we could do was to agree to be nice to each other and to respect each other's judgment. In a world where religion was so hopelessly private only mutual acceptance would do. The "I believe" of traditional religion was replaced by "I want to believe" or "I need to believe." Theology, if you only changed the vocabulary, could easily turn into a form of secular psychotherapy.

The third foundation was thisworldliness. The ritual of traditional prayer and devotion now seemed somewhat outmoded, especially in a setting where the supernatural and the afterlife were not to be taken seriously. Even where the forms of the old ritual were retained, the message was clear. Salvation was of this world. The vision of Christianity and Judaism turned to an earthly paradise of peace, plenty, love and harmony. Personal immortality may indeed exist. But it is less important than the salvation of the human race here on earth. The old gospel of sin and resurrection was replaced by the social gospel of working for the Messianic age. Social action became the liberal substitute for soul-searing repentance. Ministers and rabbis began talking more and more about love and justice and less and less about the world to come. The difference between secular utopians and liberal religionists was difficult to see.

Secular religion was especially strong in North America. The social gospel proved very attractive to the members of mainline Protestant denominations. Methodists, Presbyterians, Episcopalians, Congregationalists, Northern Baptists and Unitarians, deeply influenced by the impact of science, capitalism and secular education were very comfortable with the change. A golden age for all humanity seemed more appropriate than heavenly rewards and hellish punishments. The Jesus of the social gospel became a social reformer intent on improving human relations and inspiring a revolution of love.

Reform Judaism was the Jewish equivalent of the social gospel. It was uncomfortable with worlds to come and resurrections of the dead. Neither the *supernatural* nor *spiritual* was its cup of tea. It called for ethical action as the supreme expression of "religion." Striving for the Messianic Age on planet earth was its vision. But finding support for this focus on a secular utopia was not easy in the religious literature of the past. The Hebrew prophets were finally chosen as the spokesmen of the true Judaism, although their deep and abiding suspicion of urban life and their profound belief in the cataclysmic intervention of God into human affairs hardly seemed the stuff out of which this worldly utopia was made. Yet, despite this awkward marriage of the past with the present, Reform worked.

In time, after about sixty years, the Catholic Church followed. Vatican Council II changed the face of the Church. Latin yielded to the vernacular. The priest turned around and talked to the congregation. Lay people took over the management of parishes. Nuns put on secular clothing. The clergy put on jeans and invited the people to call them by their first names. Non-Catholics became friendly custodians of wisdom. The poor and the oppressed became heroes. The politics of the Left replaced the call for salvation. Personal conscience critiqued the pronouncements of the Pope. The social gospel was reborn, long after it had burned out among liberal Protestants and Reform Jews. Suddenly, an army of priests and nuns and Catholic lay people marched for peace, interracial understanding, feminism and welfare reform. The Church was transformed. The gospel of love replaced the expectations of heaven.

In the confrontation of much of establishment religion with the dreams of secularism, secularism was the winner. Much of modern religion gave up the next world for this world. Secular utopias replaced supernatural ones. The agenda of liberal religion and that of liberal politics became indistinguishable. Unlike prayer and worship, love and compassion are not necessarily religious.

CRISIS OF SECULARISM

Secular utopias are much more vulnerable than religious utopias. Reward and punishment in an afterlife are difficult to prove. Nobody comes back to testify about what happens. But living happily ever after on earth is open to public inspection. There is always the risk that your promises will fail, that paradise will not come. Religious utopias can survive in faith for long periods of time, even when their believers suffer intensely. But secular utopias have time limits. If they do not show up, they produce disillusionment and rejection.

What is ironic about the twentieth century is that, despite the tremendous advances in material welfare for so many millions, pessimism and disappointment are everywhere. The promises of science, capitalism and socialism were too extravagant. They raised the level of expectation too high. People imagined that peace, prosperity and happiness were just around the corner. Whatever benefits they received seemed woefully inadequate next to the utopian vocabulary of secular politics. Most of us measure progress by comparing where we are with what we have come to expect, not with what we used to have. After all the secular hype, the only possible response was disillusionment.

The belief in "progress," which was the secular equivalent of the religious afterlife, has died from disappointment. The old optimism of Enlightenment philosophers, Walt Whitman patriots, Horatio Alger devotees and Marxist revolutionaries is gone. It was crushed by terrible events and unfulfilled dreams.

People looked forward to technology. But they did not anticipate the curse of bigness, repetitive assembly line work and the unemployment that comes from automation. Technology meant power for the people at the top. But it often meant dependency, surveillance and loss of control for those at the bottom. Complaining to a computer leaves a great deal to be desired.

People looked forward to the excitement of urban living. But they did not understand what it meant to live as an isolated family or as an anonymous individual. They did not understand the possibility of pollution, violence and crime. The cruel indifference of urban strangers came as a surprise.

People expected continuing prosperity, upward and onward. They imagined that free enterprise would guarantee *goodies* for all. They were naive about economic cycles, recessions and depressions. They were over optimistic about giving power to government and the parameters of growth. Poverty and unemployment were not what they expected in utopia.

People anticipated peace. They were convinced that the hostilities and the hatreds of the past would vanish. They were surprised by two devastating world wars, the power of deadly nationalism and the invention of weapons to exterminate millions. The holocaust of victims was almost incomprehensible.

Some people imagined that the socialist revolution would usher in an era of justice and unparalleled plenty. The overthrow of the old order would lead to the classless society of equality and sharing. But paradise turned into poverty, gulags and state terror. The Marxist dream became a nightmare.

People expected utopia and they got much less than they expected. The secular dream had failed them. With the vision in tact the world had meaning. With the vision gone it began to look crazy. The philosophies of the twentieth century started to reflect this disillusionment.

Sigmund Freud, the founder of psychoanalysis, was traumatized by the terrible events of the First World War. He was overwhelmed by the suicidal self-destruction of the combatants. He tried to explain how all this aggressive killing was related to the drive for life. The energy of his pleasure principle, the libido, was the servant of life. But it now seemed opposed by a sinister psychic force that pervaded human behavior. This force was a compulsion to seek death. And this pursuit of death was as strong in the human psyche as the pursuit of life. People were the victims of an internal contradiction. They wanted both life and death simultaneously. The disharmony of the human mind seemed to reflect the disharmony of the universe.

ALIENATION

The loss of the secular dream affected the thinking of the twentieth century. Philosophers and writers gave expression to their profound sense of alienation from a world that no longer supported their desires. The universe became an adversary instead of a friend. The world of the utopias faded away and then re-appeared as a hostile stranger.

Much of what we call modernism is the work of alienation. The optimism of social transformation is replaced by brooding introspection and bizarre fantasy. The paradigm writer of disillusionment was Franz Kafka, the Czech Jewish novelist. The protagonists of his stories are men filled with self-loathing and a sense of insignificance. They feel the chill of absurdity in the powers that control their lives. As anonymous men, they confront anonymous accusers. The individual becomes a helpless bewildered object of manipulation by forces he can neither comprehend nor identify. When he suffers, he even prefers to plead guilty to unknown crimes rather than admit that the universe has no moral agenda. It is better to be guilty in a just world than to be innocent in a chaotic one. But no confession of guilt can eliminate the terror of living in world that makes no sense.

The pathetic Rubachov of Arthur Koestler's *Darkness At Noon* is a devout communist who falls victim to Stalin's anger. He is a faithful son of the Revolution, who is now falsely accused of treason. If he resists his guilt, he will have to admit to himself that the Party has failed, that the hopes and dreams of millions are illusions, that the struggle and sacrifice of the last twenty years have been for nought. And so he pleads guilty to crimes he never committed. It is better to die in a sane world where justice prevails than to live in a crazy one, where the best-laid plans of the most sincere reformers turn into nothing.

The most dramatic example of alienation is the rise of existentialism, especially in its popular French form. Both Jean Paul Satre and Albert Camus deeply distrusted the universe they were born into. It was devoid of meaning and filled with frustration and failure. The horrors of war and fascism had dismissed the illusion of utopia. Without any guarantee of success all that was left to man was his dignity. He must refuse to accept his fate. He must turn to the mindless world with defiance and proclaim his resistance.

Mersault, the protagonist of Camus' *The Stranger*, lives from day to day with supreme indifference. Even when his mother dies he displays no emotion. Even when he is sentenced to death for a crime he has not really committed, he accepts his fate with no resistance. Destiny is relentless and has its own reasons. Defiance is a useless enterprise. Only when, at the very end, he is confronted with the meaninglessness of his own death does he "wake up" to shout his anger. He is transformed. He breathes defiance. He will not accept what is unacceptable. He will not pretend that dying is of no importance. His execution is inevitable, but he will not dignify it with his indifference. The universe does not care whether he lives or dies. But *he* does. And so they are enemies.

The existentialist denies that human life has any essential purpose. We merely exist under the sentence of death. We can freely choose to accept that sentence or resist it. But we cannot escape it.

Destiny is our foe. And, although we cannot defeat it, we can preserve our dignity by never saying *yes* to it.

Life is dissonance. Nothing fits. The universe is a cruel joke. We want what we cannot have.

The world is an unfriendly indifferent place. As Camus reminds us: "Man stands, face to face with the irrational. He feels within him his longing for happiness and for reason. The absurd is born of this confrontation between the human need and the unreasonable silence of the universe." (*The Myth of Sisyphus*) Or, as David Hume complained: "The life of man is of no greater importance to the universe than that of an oyster." (*Essays/ "Of Suicide"*)

DESPERATION

Some thinkers find this alienation too distressing. They accept a world with no guarantees. But they prefer to view it in a more positive light. If they cannot have a just and omnipotent God, they are willing to settle for a just and limited one. Instead of viewing the world as half empty, it is better to view the world as half full.

Both John Dewey, the father of progressive education and Mordecai Kaplan, the founder of Reconstructionist Judaism, redefined God in order to perceive him as a symbol of hope and legitimate human aspiration. Their God is a secular God, operating through natural law and dreaming only thisworldly dreams. His virtue is that he is all good. His limitation is that he is not able to do everything he wants to do. Instead of an all-powerful father, he is a supportive friend. Evil exists but is not part of God. What is good is God, even though there is not enough of it.

Now a secular religion with a limited God may not be as wonderful as a supernatural religion with an all-powerful Deity. But it seems to be better than alienation. If we cannot have the whole universe on our side, at least having part of the universe on our side is some consolation.

Harold Kushner seems to think so. He is a "disciple" of Mordecai Kaplan. He is also the author of the bestseller *When Bad Things Happen To Good People*. When his young son fell victim to progeria, a disease of premature aging, his faith in God, even a this-worldly God, was badly shaken. How could a just and loving providence condemn an innocent child to suffering and early death? It all seemed so unfair. But not believing in God, not believing in some good force out there was emotionally unacceptable to him. He would rather have some weak but good God than not to have any God at all. The thought that God cared, even though he was not able to save the child, eased the pain of abandonment and helplessness. Maybe a God that got an *A* for effort was just as good as a God that got an *A* for performance.

Kushner's answer is an understandable one. But it is not a satisfactory one. God is important, not only because he is good, but especially because he is powerful, especially because he can guarantee good things. If He is as helpless as we are, how significant are his good intentions? A meaningful universe is not a universe of good intentions. It is a universe of good results. Knowing that God is also frustrated provides little comfort. It only means that alienation is divine, as well as human.

A secular religion that still believes in utopia has power. But a secular religion that settles for good intentions simply means that we have to look for better answers elsewhere.

4

NEW SEARCH FOR MEANING

THE CRISIS OF TRADITIONAL religion and secular utopianism has produced a third alternative. It is the most popular form of liberal religion around. Its devotees call it New Age Thinking.

New Age Thinking exists because people want a meaningful universe. They want a world in which human hopes and human reality fit one with the other. They want a world which is more harmonious than the way it initially appears. But they want a philosophy of life that will not take away the freedom which science and capitalism have given them. They want an approach to living that is more poetic and more spiritual than secular thinking.

Traditional religion emphasized faith. Secular utopians put their trust in reason. New Age thinkers are comfortable with intuition.

Both faith and reason may be confirmed by intuition. But they are not the same thing. Intuition is a combination of direct knowing and feeling that seems to carry its own justification. Sometimes the conclusions of intuition are conservative, supporting the status quo. Sometimes they are radical, driving rebels to challenge established values and to overthrow established institutions. Both Friedrich Nietzsche and Albert Camus were radical intuitionists.

The revelations of intuition are something like "aha, that's it!" We bump into the truth and know that it is the truth even though we cannot explain why. An overwhelming feeling of certainty accompanies our deepest intuitions. Unlike faith we are not restricted by the traditions of our ancestors. Unlike reason we do not need to rely on measurable evidence. In the realm of ethics and morality intuition turns into conscience. We know what is right, not because it is found in an ancient book, not because it has appropriate consequences, but because it conforms to our deepest perceptions.

Intuition is more romantic than reason. It is wonderfully spontaneous. It is filled with surprise. It is not tied down to tedious research and pedestrian measurement. It is infused with feeling and emotion. It is even "mysterious" never really explaining why we know what we know. Above all it is personal, individual and subjective. Nobody else can tell me what I feel. Nobody else can experience what I experience.

Intuition is also more romantic than faith. Traditional faith is connected to authoritarian religion, rigid conformity and repetitive ritual. It is more comfortable with obedience and humility than with creative insight and subjective wisdom. If intuition is allowed to roam freely it may find its way to outrageous and non-traditional conclusions. Intuitionists may end up by saying that all religions are equally true, or that nature is God, or even that people are God.

Most mystics belong to this intuitionist and romantic circle of truth-seekers. They want a direct connection to God. They want to experience, not just hear about, the power of the divine. Spirituality is more important to them than formal religion. Ecstasy is more meaningful than dogmas or creeds. Jewish, Christian, Muslim and Hindu mystics have always been a threat to the religious establishment.

The romantic movements of modern times start with this personal and intimate way of discovering reality. They are deeply suspicious of reason, with its detached and analytic way of approaching reality. They are impatient with religious dogma, with its institutional and credal restrictions on the human spirit. They want something "deeper" than rationality and "freer" than faith. They are searching for that direct and immediate experience that proves life and the universe are meaningful.

All romantics were united in their rejection of both the Enlightenment and dogmatic religion. They preferred the free spirit to the disciplines of either tradition or science, and the possibility of mystery to matter-of-fact knowledge. Some of them, like Rousseau, imagined that "primitive" man was more in tune with reality than the sophisticated savants of modern society. Maybe, when life is simple, people are closer to the truth of nature.

In time the romantic impulse was confronted by a dilemma. Does the meaning of life lie in the freedom of the free spirit? Or does it lie in the universe which the free spirit discovers? Nietzsche opted for the freedom of the free spirit. The world is a story of endless repetition and suffering, a meaningless world in which nothing lasts and all glory fades away. But the human spirit resists this fate. It surges forth to make its statement, to affirm its power, to put the force of human will against the indifference of nature. The free spirit finds meaning in its freedom and power. It shuns all limits, whether the commands of God or the structures of conventional morality. It is ridiculous to judge Alexander the Great or Napoleon by normal standards. Their achievements transcend the narrow categories of narrow people.

Modern existentialism picked up some of this Nietzschean passion. The universe of Jean-Paul Sartre and Albert Camus may be morally absurd and without meaning. But the human spirit is divine in its freedom. Man may not be God. But he is more than predictable urges and programmed behavior. People are free and responsible the way God, if he exists, is free and responsible. Science and reason may claim that every event must have a cause, that the laws of nature are the iron laws of fate, that all of us live in the prison of determinism from which we cannot escape. But the intuition of consciousness and self-awareness gives the lie to this cynicism. We are free in a way that the rest of the world is not free. That is both our glory and our burden. We are not the discoverers of meaning. We are the authors of meaning through the choices we make.

The human hero, standing alone but free, is the role model of the romantic existentialist. But it is not the only romantic possibility or the most attractive. The free spirit in a lonely and unfriendly universe may indulge the heady emotion of defiance. But it is still acting out its defiance in a lonely and unfriendly universe. How much better it would be if intuition could give us what we really want, a supportive and friendly cosmos.

Enter mysticism. The mystic experience is an old one attested to by countless holy men and women within the established religions. Mystics all over the world share a perception of the universe which transcends local boundaries. In the end, the experience of Christian mystics is not substantially different from the experiences of Jewish, Muslim, Hindu and Buddhist mystics. They all testify to the same "reality." This is the direct experience of a cosmic consciousness, which is God. There is the deep awareness that all things in the universe are parts of a greater whole, which is infused with beauty and harmony. There is the knowledge that all the world is good and that all events which happen in the world, if seen from the perspective of cosmic consciousness, are also good. There is the overwhelming sense that the human spirit and God are really one.

When religion is unorganized, mysticism is very popular. But when it becomes organized it poses a danger. Mystics have a tendency to bypass the religious establishment and make their own direct contact with God. The messages they receive are not always consistent with the prevailing dogma; and their reliance on personal experience tends to undermine traditional authority. Spirituality replaces ritual and ethics as the heart of religion. The spiritual experience is more open and all-embracing than religious politics is comfortable with. When you are experiencing God directly, statements *about* God seem less than compelling.

Although mystics were fashionable among Christians, Jews and Muslims, the emergence of science and capitalism in the West tended to make them unfashionable. Reason and analysis did not seem compatible with ecstatic experiences of cosmic consciousness. Spirituality took a back seat to social ethics as the heart of the religious enterprise. But in Eastern religion, in the world of Hinduism and Buddhism, the mystic retained his pre-eminent position. Holy men and women, monks and nuns, remained role models of human aspiration. Both poverty and social stagnation encouraged withdrawal from the outer world of pain and suffering to an inner world of peace and harmony. The cruel world was not to be remade and refashioned. It was to be transcended.

Already in the nineteenth century European romantics had discovered the spirituality of the East. The conquest of India and China by Western powers brought Western secular culture to the East. But it also exposed European visitors to the mysticism of Hinduism and Buddhism. By the end of the nineteenth century Vedanta and theosophical ideas had penetrated the cultural centers of the West, especially among intellectuals and romantics who found no pleasure in the technological achievements of capitalist culture, and who resented the dogmatic limitations of Western religion. Not burdened by the religious politics of the East, Western romantics could extract from Eastern philosophy whatever was appealing and discard what was unattractive. Very much as Chinese food was embraced by Westerners and adapted to the Western palate, so a "sanitized" Eastern mysticism entered the Western world and found a large receptive audience.

Eastern mysticism in the West was not burdened with elaborate rituals, dogmatic priesthoods and racist castes. It could present itself as a "pure" philosophy of religious experience, untainted by all the ills of organized religion. It became an individual choice, which ran counter to the secular rational trends of Western culture and which carried no old offensive institutional baggage. While in India it was imbedded in a repressive social system; in America it was identified with personal freedom and exploration. For people no longer satisfied with the religious and secular answers of the Western world, it emerged as a fresh alternative.

The Age of Aquarius began in the sixties during the turmoil of the Vietnam War and civil rights movement. Old authority and old institutions were collapsing. Affluence and mobility had undermined family traditions and cohesiveness. The confidence of the Anglosax-on establishment was shaken. Individual freedom and personal rebel-lion were easy options. The quest for meaning became a popular agony, intensified by rising expectations and by a growing sense of frustration with politics and social revolution. The spiritual option became increasingly attractive, especially if it came dressed up in exot-ic clothing and with promises of personal power.

The new spirituality was obviously a rejection of the old secular utopianism; but it was not a revival of the old religion. In fact, many New Age people did not like the word "religion." They pre-ferred the world "spiritual" as a more open term which focused on personal experience rather than denominational beliefs.

> Jerry is a former Roman Catholic who drifted away from his childhood church because he did not like the dogma. He was an atheist and Marxist for a while, active in student politics and naively expectant of salvation through political action. By the mid-seventies he was disillusioned with activism but still filled with idealism and searching. Going back to his old church had no appeal for him. He was looking for something "deeper," "more profound," "more universal" and "more personal." He was one of the first recruits of the Age of Aquarius. He put together his own package of mind power, Zen and holistic healing. He now reads all the time from the books of the new spiritual masters. He attends weekend retreats sponsored by groups that promise "self-actualization" and "peak experiences." He has inte-grated meditation and yoga into his daily routine. He shies away from organizational commitments. His spiritual jour-ney is "my very own."

The new spirituality is very different from the old religion. It recruits millions of people who have no need for denominational labels or community commitments. It finds truth and spiritual awareness in all religions. It has no difficulty in blending ideas from Hinduism with modern psychotherapy or Taoism with native American philosophy. It is impatient with creeds and religious authorities and makes its appeal to personal experience. Sensual pleasures and sexuality are not embarrassments. Thisworldliness and transcendence cooperate as partners. The language of modern science is merged with the language of mysticism. Above all, the final judge of what to do and where to go is the individual. If spiritual wisdom is God, then God speaks to us directly.

One of the most charismatic of the Aquarian thinkers was Joseph Campbell. A famous writer, teacher and lecturer, he became America's most distinguished mythologist. Influenced by the spiritual teachers of both East and West, he emerged as the most successful spokesman for the new spirituality. Just before his death a series of interviews with Bill Moyers made him a television star and presented his ideas to millions of viewers. Handsome, articulate and brilliant, he became the voice of the "post-rational" world. The transcript of his conversation with Moyers, *The Power of Myth*, became a nationwide best seller. There was something about Campbell's message that was enormously appealing, that struck a responsive chord in the hearts and minds of so many of his listeners and readers.

The message of Joseph Campbell is the quintessential message of New Age spirituality.

Here was a man who was initially familiar with all the religious traditions of the past, who had mastered the ideas and wisdom of modern anthropology and psychology who could hold his own in the formal setting of the academic classroom or in the coziness of the communal tub at the Esalen Institute, a rebel against the dogmatic narrowness of his Irish Roman Catholic childhood, who still loved the beauty and mystery of the rituals of his youth. His spiritual odyssey moved from traditional religion through secular science into the world of the Aquarian free spirit. When Campbell spoke, he addressed the "eternal question." Does the world have any meaning? Does life have any meaning?

The Campbell answer goes something like this: There are two ways of experiencing the world. The first is narrowly rational and analytic. It sees the world as filled with conflict, confrontation and disharmony. The second way is spiritual and synthetic. It perceives intuitively and deeply that behind the apparent disharmony, there exists a fundamental unity and harmony. This ground of being is not outside nature. It pervades it in the very same way that the soul pervades the body. From the perspective of cosmic consciousness all opposites are reconciled, all contradictions resolved.

When the world is analyzed and divided up into parts it appears to be ugly and unjust. But when it is experienced as a whole it reveals itself to be beautiful and good. The spiritual eye is superior to the rational eye. And the spiritual experience is more meaningful than any analytic insight. Rationality distorts, but the spiritual vision enables us to see the truth.

Spiritual truth does not come from experience. It comes from within our soul, from the very depths of our unconscious mind. We are born with all the spiritual wisdom we need to know for personal fulfillment. But we often forget that we have it and search for evidence outside ourselves. If only we could hear and experience the messages from deep within ourselves, they would guide us to the light and help us see the splendor and meaningfulness of the universe.

The path to truth is an inner voyage as much as it is a confrontation with danger and challenge. The hero with a thousand faces is the central figure of a thousand religions. He is Moses, Jesus, Mohammed, Krishna and Buddha. He travels far and wide to find the truth and then discovers that it was always there, deep within himself. The moment of enlightenment is when he discovers the unity of all things, the "love" that binds all things together. In such a "revelation" the hunter and the hunted are no longer adversaries. They are joined together by a bond of mutual consent. Life devours life in order that life may continue. Death is not the enemy of life. It is an episode in its transformation.

Every person has his own "hero," his own path to enlightenment, deep within himself. Every path is individual. No one else has exactly the same road to truth. Others may guide us to wisdom. But they cannot tell us what to experience and what to do. Only our own personal inner voice can serve as our ultimate guru. Dogmatic religions which insist on one path and one way for everybody undermine spirituality. The spirit must be free to find its own way in accordance with its own light. It must follow its own bliss.

But, in the end, although there are many personal roads to wisdom, the destination is the same. The truth that surpasses all understanding is the place where the hero arrives. This peak experience is not confined to life after death or to misty mountain tops. It may happen in the most ordinary of places with the most ordinary of people. Nor is it a final destination with nothing to follow. Spiritual experiences come and go. But when they happen, the world is perceived in a different way. What seemed crazy and disconnected in our lives now seems appropriate and fitting. What was divided now becomes whole. What appeared to be unfair and unjust now seems to be part of a greater harmony. We see the world through the lens of cosmic consciousness and we know that it is a good.

Lori has discovered the wonders of spirituality. She was very depressed after a painful divorce and after her only child moved two thousand miles away to Los Angeles, to "find himself." She experienced her life as a failure and felt victimized by forces over which she exercised no control. Life became bleak and uninteresting. She avoided friends. She withdrew into herself. One day she was given a book of verses by the charismatic Hindu mystic Krishnamurti. After she read it, she claimed that her life was transformed. She turned to meditation, yoga and disciplined introspection. She "devoured" books on Eastern philosophy and mysticisms. She attended weekend marathons for spiritual awareness. Names like Ram Dass, Muktananda, and Jean Huston fell increasingly from her lips. She claimed that her depression had vanished and that she now felt very much "centered," very much open to the inner voices which had always been there but which she had never been able to hear before. Her outward bitterness vanished. She became less angry and anxious. She spoke of extraordinary experiences where she felt ecstatically merged with some transcendent yet immanent presence so overwhelming that the ordinary boundaries of her ego vanished and she felt completely at one with the universe. She even spoke of an intense light that appeared in one of her visions, so compelling that it drew her to it irresistibly and filled her being with a sense that at the heart of everything was this shining goodness. Lori, like thousands of others, has found the path of spirituality. She is convinced that this path is the true path to happiness, self-fulfillment and peace of mind. While she concedes that every person has to find her own way to spiritual wisdom, no other experience can give true meaning to life. It is only the spiritual experience that enables people to see and to feel the fundamental goodness that underlies all reality, even events that, from the ordinary perspective of daily living, are normally outrageous. Spirituality has nothing to do with organized religion. It is a personal and private voyage, guided by teachers, and independent of any institutional and dogmatic requirement. Lori now finds traditional religion to be "too narrow" and "too literal." She condemns liberal religion as "too concerned with social issues" and too little concerned with personal spiritual development. She finds rational and scientific approaches to life as "too cold" and "too sterile." She is especially contemptuous of "left-brain personalities" who are too analytic and who never tune into the synthetic spiritual messages coming from the right-brain. Her insistence on being right seems to indicate that perhaps she is less comfortable with life than her personal testimony would indicate. But it is hard to challenge her because all her evidence is internal and subjective.

Lori's personal odyssey can be multiplied by thousands. Many, many people have been deeply influenced by New Age mysticism. They are convinced that their spiritual experiences have transformed their lives and brought meaning to their existence. Some claim that their spiritual power can cure disease, divine the future, control pain and direct nature. Others claim paranormal powers that include extra-sensory perception, clairvoyance, out-of-body experiences and communication with the dead. But all maintain that spirituality is the foundation of happiness, fulfillment and sanity.

ROMANTIC HYPE

Despite the seductiveness of Aquarian thinking, many thoughtful people have reservations about the claims of this romantic "movement." There are the obvious skeptics who may not discount spirituality but who have difficulty believing in talking to the dead and having out-of-body experiences. There are the naturalists who are perfectly willing to recognize "paranormal" powers but who claim that there is a natural explanation for them. If there is extra-sensory perception, if some people can really detect the thoughts of others, that power does not rest in some mysterious spiritual force. It arises from some discrete measurable energy, like all the other energies which science investigates. If there really is psychic healing, if the mind can help cure physical illness, that power does not reflect some fundamental difference between mind and body. The power of the mind is the power of the brain. And the brain is made out of matter—an extraordinary arrangement of atoms and molecules—but still matter.

But the fundamental argument is with the experience of spirituality itself and what it means. No one can deny that people have spiritual experiences or that they are ecstatic or wonderful or that they make people feel good and give them peace of mind. Yet to "jump" from this experience to the knowledge that all is well with the world is a leap of faith that no experience, however powerful, can justify. Feeling at one with the universe happens often, even to people who do not think of themselves as either mystical or spiritual. After all, biology tells us that we are intimately related to all living things; and physics teaches us that the atoms of our bodies are the same as the atoms of the universe. But feeling at one with the universe cannot demonstrate that all the events of the universe happen for the good and that they all exist in some perfect harmony. Even the experience of an intense white light is just that—an experience of an intense white light. It cannot make evil less evil.

It may be the case that the agenda of the killer and the agenda of the killed are in some mysterious way, united in an ultimate harmony. But tell that to the innocent child assaulted by a deadly virus. Tell that to the terrified chicken pursued by the hungry farmer.

The absurdity of a crazy world cannot be canceled out by unrelated wonderful experiences. The glow of peak experiences simply means that, amid this world of highs and lows, there are wonderful happenings. It cannot demonstrate that all things are wonderful. The intuition of the right brain may help us to see what the pragmatic left-brain may not notice. But it cannot turn pain into pleasure, nor evil into good. The whole may be more than the sum of its parts. Yet, it is not possible for any human being to experience the whole universe. We may feel at one with nature. We may experience our spirit transcending our body and floating through outer space. But everything we encounter is only a fragment, even though a larger fragment, of the universe.

There is something called "romantic hype." "Romantic hype" loves exaggeration. It cannot allow special moments to be special moments. It cannot allow beauty to be simply beauty. It cannot allow ecstasy to be simply ecstasy. It needs to expand their significance beyond what they normally are. Like falling in love for the first time the lover needs to see the beloved as the be-all and end-all of existence.

"Romantic hype" goes beyond what intuition reveals. It is drawn by the desperate need to give meaning to the world. It cannot settle for modest answers and good-humored uncertainty. It wants every intense experience to have cosmic significance. Finding some useful wisdom through introspection means getting in touch with the collective universe. Enjoying restful meditation means discovering the path to enlightenment and salvation. Dancing ecstatically to the rhythms of native American music means experiencing the vibrations of the universe.

Henry is a young man who attended a marathon weekend at the ashram of a California guru. He claims that he learned more about life and the world in those three days than in all the previous twenty years of his formal education. His joy and exaltation are evident. When asked what he learned he replies with great seriousness that he has discovered that "All is Love." He explains that he now knows that everything in the universe is bound together by the force of love, even the atoms of his body, even the electrons and protons of the atoms. Love is the most powerful energy in the world. If only one can tune into that energy, there is no obstacle that cannot be transcended, no disease that cannot be cured. Henry speaks about his profound unbelievable intense moment of revelation when he held hands with others in the quiet of community meditation. There was an irresistible stream of love rising from the very depths of his being, over-flowing his spirit and embracing all the people in the room. It was as though some transcendent energy had entered his body, overwhelmed his sense of separateness and united him with everybody and everything around him. At that moment he understood that love was at the very center of exis-tence. From that moment on he felt light and joyous—and the terrible headaches which had plagued him for the past nine years vanished.

What does Henry's experience mean? No one can deny that Henry had undergone a profound experience that weekend. No one can deny that Henry felt an overpowering and intense love for the people who were near him, or that he felt bound to them with a power that he had never experienced before. No one can deny that his headaches had vanished. But no one rational can figure out what that has to do with atoms loving each other or with the force of love as the major energy of the universe. All that was demonstrated by Henry's experience was that feelings of love can sometimes be overwhelming and that sometimes they can be good for you. Turning a single personal experience into a cosmic commentary is illegitimate. It is nothing more than "romantic hype."

Many of the charms of Aquarian thinking go beyond what the "spiritual experience" can possibly point to. Romantics often want their personal experiences of happenings and healing to be more than personal or even human. They want the whole universe to be as "happy" as they are. But their assertion is a leap of faith no different from that of traditional religion. In the end neither faith, reason nor instruction can remove the "craziness" of a "crazy" world. There may be love in the world. But the whole world is not loving.

5

REALISM

When I was very young I was given a blue Parker pen as a birthday gift. It was very sleek and beautiful and since I enjoyed handwriting, it was very special to me. I guarded it with my life. One day a student in my class, a girl I barely knew, ran up to me while I was sitting on the school steps. She asked to borrow my pen to write something down, since she could not find her own pen. I was reluctant to give it to her. But I did not want to appear selfish or fussy. I gave it to her. A few minutes later I heard a scream. I turned to see her standing almost paralyzed with the open pen in her hand. "I dropped it" she shouted and then walked over to me, handed me the pen and said, without looking me in the eye, "I'm sorry." I was too stunned to ask her what happened. I simply looked at the bent nib, destroyed from its collision with the sidewalk. In a moment my most precious possession had been destroyed. The perpetrator of the "crime" had moved on with her friends, totally uninterested in my distress. I felt so much despair and anger that I started to cry. One of my teachers passed by. She was an old spinster whom nobody liked except me. I liked her because she always displayed a certain rough strength and consistency of purpose that made me feel that I was not wasting my time when I listened to her. She saw me fighting back my tears and came over to me, and, much to my surprise, put her arm around my shoulders and asked me what was wrong. Although embarrassed by my inability to control my tears, I explained to her how unfair I thought it was that my beautiful pen should be destroyed, in a moment, by somebody who did not even care. I told her that I was so mad that all I could do was cry. She turned me around, bent down to look at me face to face and said, with that special direct way she had that made you trust her sincerity, "Sherwin, the world is unfair. Being mad at it and crying won't change it. You pen is broken and you didn't deserve to have it broken. So dry your tears and be strong. If you do you will find that you are stronger then you think."

I must confess that I was a little taken back by what she said to me. I would have preferred at the time if she had hugged me and told me to go ahead and just cry. But, as the years have gone by, I have never forgotten what she said. In its own harsh way, it summed up what staying sane in a crazy world is all about.

Being strong is being rational. Being rational is being realistic. Realism is the courage to look the world square in the face and not turn away. It is the power to stop crying and whining and raging when the world "misbehaves." It is the ability to start with what is and then move on to what ought to be without having to pretend that what is has already, in some mysterious way, become what ought to be.

Realism has no patience with artful ways to dodge reality. It understands why religious tradition is so strong and so powerful; but it does not allow old books and venerable advice to interfere with the evidence of experience. It understands why philosophers and politicians invent utopias that can never exist; but it does not need the hype of absurd promises to provide the momentum for living. It understands why the mystery of spiritual power and spiritual wisdom is so romantically appealing; but it is reluctant to turn people into gods.

BASIC TRUTHS

Realism starts with the recognition of certain basic truths.

The world has a reality all its own

The world is not a figment of my imagination, a projection of my desire, a personal preserve where my emotions can invent a place they need to live in. It is something external to me, out there, objective, independent of whether I want it or do not want it, like it or do not like it. The world is too big for me to control all of it, or most of it. But the most fundamental intuition of being alive is recognizing that it is there, separate from me and filled with agendas that are not my own.

When I was in college I once entered into an absurd debate with a self-proclaimed "solipsist." He told me, at a midnight discussion in the dormitory, that he could not prove that anything existed outside his own mind. My first response was that if he truly

believed that—and I doubted that he did—he would not be responding to me as passionately as he did. You do not scream at something
you believe to be only the invention of your own mind. The human
mind is not the world. It is only a small part of it. We cannot
invent the reality that we want. We have to live with the reality that is.

Unpleasant facts are as real as pleasant facts

Facts are events. Like space and time they flow into one another. But
they are there for us to bump into. If we want to, we can regard the
whole universe as one big event. But that perspective is not very
useful given the human agenda. First, we cannot experience the universe as a whole. And second, even if we could, it is not clear that it
would give us a spiritual high instead of a headache.

Facts are morally neutral. They just happen. They bear no
intrinsic value. Their value is a relative matter. What is useful for one
person may not be useful to another. What may be pleasant to one living being may not be pleasant to another. Humans love the sun, bats
do not. Chimpanzees fancy termites, but termites do not fancy
chimpanzees.

What is quite clear from the human perspective, is that the
universe is filled with facts that are both pleasant and unpleasant. Red
suns set on tropical horizons. Happy babies are born to ecstatic
mothers. Falling in love transforms the lives of men and women. The
world can be a wonderful place to live in. But it also can be a terrible
place to live in. Innocent children are shot to death on inner city
streets. Young people die from painful diseases. Old people decay into
helplessness.

Pleasant facts are real. But they are no more real than unpleasant facts. Seeing the good in the world is no more profound than seeing the evil. In fact, the structure of the human psyche is such that

we notice danger before we tune into what is safe and supportive. We have to make an effort to notice the positive things in life. But that effort does not make the positive side of living more significant.

I recently paid a condolence call on a grieving widow who lost her young husband to pancreatic cancer. They had been very much in love. And the loss for her was overwhelming. Her aunt, who was trying to be supportive, said to her, "You know, you had twelve wonderful years together. You have marvelous memories. You have to focus on the positive." The widow burst into tears. The aunt had obviously said the wrong thing. She was unaware that the twelve wonderful years were the reason why the tragedy was so tragic. Had they been twelve rotten years, had the husband been an insensitive boor, the widow's loss would have been insignificant.

Pain is all the more terrible when it follows pleasure that is all the more wonderful. Life would be easier if it did not have the highs and lows. The highness of the highs does not diminish or compensate for the lowness of the lows. Losing a baby you love does not become more tolerable because you had him for three marvelous months. It becomes only more unbearable. It is as though the fates tease us with happiness and then withdraw it after we are addicted.

We may choose to risk the pain of tragic loss by committing ourselves to love. The experience is worth the risk. But the loss is no less terrible because warm memories survive, especially when natural hopes and expectations have been dashed, especially when you feel cheated or feel that your loved one has been cheated.

The world is filled with many incompatible agendas

Many people ask "What is the purpose of life?" or "What is the purpose of the universe?" The question implies that there is a *single* overreaching goal to the world, and we need to find out what it is. It also implies that all the goals of all the conscious or unconscious beings in the universe are mutually compatible and fit neatly into some harmonious spiritual whole.

Leisure fishermen think of fishing as a restful, peaceful activity in which they can escape the hustle and bustle of urban living and feel in harmony with nature and at one with the world. But for the fish, fishing is never restful nor peaceful. If they get caught, they die after a painful struggle. Perhaps some fish psychologist can demonstrate that the fish derive great satisfaction and well-being from getting caught, killed and eaten. But I doubt it. Fishing for fish, is a horrible experience a confrontation of the human agenda with the fish agenda. What is peace and calm for one being is terror and trauma for another.

Of course, one can always maintain that God made fish so that men could catch them, and eat them. The trauma of the fish fits into the overreaching purpose of God. But that piece of news does not make it any easier for the fish. It just adds a third agenda, God's agenda, to the confrontation. Maybe fish ought to be enthusiastic about doing what God wants them to do. But, no matter how you cut it, the experience of becoming a fish fillet is not the stuff out of which fish dreams are made.

In the end, it is not possible to find a single agenda, even God's agenda, which absorbs, merges and encompasses the universe. The fragile organic surface of this planet is teaming with trillions of competing drives, goals and purposes. That is the savage story of evolution. Dinosaurs, by their extinction, may have made way for mammals and humans—and this may have been "progress" and consistent with the "will" of nature—but they did not go gracefully. To the end they struggled to live, regardless of what "destiny" had in store for them.

Even within the human species there is no single agenda. And even within the individual human psyche conflicting authorities compete with each other. Freud pointed out: "We are warned by a proverb against serving two masters at the same time. The poor ego has things even worse. It serves three masters and does what it can to bring their claims and demands into harmony with one another. Its three tyrannical masters are the external world, the superego (conscience) and the id (the pleasure principle)." (*New Introductory Lectures on Psychoanalysis*)

The confusion of the human mind is a reflection of the "confusion" of the universe.

Needing to believe is not enough

Carl is a student in philosophy. He is taking a course about the ideas of the great German philosopher, Immanuel Kant. Kant clearly demonstrated that it was impossible to prove either the existence or non-existence of God. Carl was raised in a devout Lutheran home. He is both attracted to and troubled by secular philosophy. He is very uncomfortable with the Kant conclusion. He challenges the Kant thesis. A heated discussion follows. After a half-hour of failing to convince his classmates, he shouts out, "I don't care whether you can prove or disprove the existence of God, I believe in God because I *need* to believe in God."

It is one thing to believe in God because the evidence of your experience and the experience of others leads you to that belief—or because you have an unconscious need to believe. But it is another thing to "believe" because you consciously choose to believe, knowing that your choice is the result of weakness, and the inability to live with uncertainty. "I need to believe" is a translation of "I am not strong enough to live with what evidence presents. If my experience does not demonstrate that something I want to believe is true, then I will pretend that it is true." How does one consciously admit to that weakness and retain one's self-respect?

Twenty-two years ago I took my first trip to the Soviet Union. Before I left I made contact with a longtime Marxist radical who had important friends in Moscow whom I wanted to interview. He had never given up his faith in the greatness of Stalin and in the wonderful achievements of the Bolshevik Revolution. Although he was an old frail man, he spoke passionately. He loved to talk and reminisced about his Party days. After about two hours of monologue, he asked how I felt about the Soviet Union. When I pointed to the incontrovertible evidence of Stalinist brutality and Russian economic stagnation, he admitted that there were problems and that terrible atrocities had been committed. But he maintained that Stalin had no other choice but to do what he did. "You see," he said pleadingly, "I am a very old radical. And it is not possible for me to give up what I committed my whole life to believing." At that point my respect for his integrity vanished. Only pity remained.

Needing to believe is no justification for believing. Knowing that you need to believe and "choosing" to believe even when you are aware that reality does not support your choice, is a form of self-depreciation. The first test of strength is the strength to face reality, no matter where the evidence leads—even if it leads to the overturning of our most cherished beliefs even if it leads to the rethinking of our whole life. Only in that foundation can true courage rest.

A meaningless world is a distinct possibility

Some people need to be hit over the head time after time before they realize that they are being hit over the head. Some people never recognize disaster because the pain of acknowledging it is worse then the pain of enduring it.

It may be the case that the answers of traditional religion, secular utopianism and spirituality are true. It may be the case that we live in a meaningful world in which all events ultimately happen for some good purpose or lead inevitably to some good end.

But it may also be the case that we live in a meaningless world, a world in which no guiding providence or justice prevails, a world in which what we give is not necessarily what we receive. So much of human experience points to this reality that it is hard to discard it as a reasonable option.

So often we fight the facts because they do not fit into our preconceived notions of reality, because reality does not conform to what we want or need. We cease to be rational. We begin to rationalize. Rationalization is finding reasons for not being reasonable. It is looking at facts through lenses distorted by desire.

My radio has just reported the death of twelve young skydivers in a freak airplane accident. Were they lucky skydivers who found the pleasure of immortality long before their friends would have a chance to? Had they chosen a life with a short-life span after a previous existence and were now waiting expectantly for a new reincarnation adventure? Were they simply a predestined chapter in airplane advancement, prompting improvements in airplane safety by their sacrifice? Or were they simply twelve unlucky people cut down by the absurdity of coincidence?

If you are strong enough to accept the last statement, you have stopped apologizing.

Painful truth is better in the end than painless fantasy

Some people prefer the world of fantasy. Why not? Why live in the real world if the real world is nasty, brutish and unjust. A strong case can be made for choosing to spend our time with illusion. Illusions can shield us from the pain of reality.

The bedraggled heroine of Woody Allen's *Purple Rose of Cairo*, living in the troubled times of the Great Depression, prefers the sheltered fantasies of the local cinema to the grind of daily life. The movies of the Depression were marvelous. The vulnerable poor, ground down by poverty and hopelessness, could retreat to parlors of opulence where the likes of Cary Grant and Katherine Hepburn could frolic in luxury on the screen and make everybody in the audience believe that they too were part of an upper class adventure. Why not pretend that life is like the movies instead of the painful struggle that it is?

A friend of mine said to me, "Realism is a form of masochism. We turn life into homework. We insist that it is good to face the facts no matter what the consequences. And our reward—a harsh, meaningless world. No thank you."

Jews before the Holocaust had to face the same alternative. If extermination and incineration were inevitable why not pretend that they were not going to happen? Many were in Germany and in occupied Europe and did exactly that. They sensed that something terrible was taking place but they preferred to deny it. It seemed silly to be paralyzed with fear when there was nothing that you could do about your fear. It was much better to imagine that you were being transported to a work camp than to a gas chamber. The final horror was bad enough without the pain of anticipation.

But the truth of the matter was that realism did make a positive differences. Jews who forced themselves to accept the future that the facts painted escaped in time or fled to safety. Awareness of what was in store for them made them change their behavior. Knowing that someone is going to kill you may scare you. But it also enables you to utilize your energies to escape or to confront.

The Klein family fled Germany in 1936. The father was a prosperous dress manufacturer in Berlin. His ancestors had come from Bohemia and had lived in Germany for over eight centuries. He himself was a decorated veteran of World War I and had been exempted from the first harsh retributions of the Nazi regime. When he decided to emigrate in 1936 his parents and siblings tried to dissuade him. They saw Hitler as a passing political fancy. They were reluctant to give up home, wealth and status for an uncertain future. But he was convinced that the Nazis had wide and strong appeal and that Hitler would do exactly what he promised to do in his book *Mein Kampf*. Against persistent family pressure he left Germany for America. He sold his business to his employees for almost nothing. He arrived penniless in America. His wife an elegant lady, was forced to open a small restaurant in her home in order to support her husband and children. But as the father said, "We are still alive. My family was killed because they refused to face the truth."

Denying painful reality makes a difference. It prevents us from acknowledging the dangers that threaten us. It makes us hide from opportunities that can save us. It gives us a false sense of security when we ought to be nervous.

Illusions never fully take over our awareness. Painful facts are hidden under the surface of our consciousness, always ready to intrude when our defenses are down. Experience cannot be dismissed from our mind by either determination or pretense. It insists on lingering. Sometime the longer we deny the dangers that surround us the stronger is our awareness of them. Fanatical beliefs of personal salvation and well-being are frequently desperate attempts to drown out the voices of doubt and fear that come from our subconscious mind. Pretending goes only so far.

Strength comes from training

The power to confront reality and not run away does not happen all by itself. It needs to be cultivated. It requires active training. People are not strong because they want to be strong. People are strong because they have mobilized their energies and channeled them through specific skills.

Strength does not come through a sudden moment of conversion. Telling yourself that you are strong does not make you strong. Just as telling yourself that you are worthwhile does not make you feel worthwhile.

The desire for strength does not produce strength. It is only the beginning. What follows is a training program for living with courage.

PART TWO

TEN STEPS
TO SANITY

6

DISMISSING ILLUSIONS
Step I

REALISM BEGINS WITH THE
refusal to stop fighting the facts.

Illusions stem from two sources. The first, and most obvious
one, is ignorance. We do not know the truth because we have not been
presented with the evidence or because we have looked at the evidence
and have misunderstood it.

Many people change their minds because they encounter facts
that are irresistible. Before Magellan, most people believed that the
earth was flat, under a flat heaven and over a flat hell. Before Coper-
nicus and Galileo, most people believed that the earth was the center
of the universe. Before Darwin, almost all people believed that

humanity and the animal world had no fundamental connection. Before Einstein, educated opinion maintained that matter and energy were distinct and separate. Before Freud, the students of the mind gave primary power to conscious thought and conscious will. Over the centuries public opinion has been forced to take paths it initially resisted. The pioneers who spoke were denounced for their ideas. But their ideas prevailed because the facts, however disturbing to confront, were on their side.

On the personal level, people also change because the facts they encounter are irresistible. Many husbands and wives terminate loveless relationships because they can no longer deny the reality of the hate and abuse they endure. Many students change the course of their study because they can see that what they want to be does not conform to what they are best able to do. Many friendships grow, after initial resistance, because the nurturing and support are so obviously genuine. Many people revise their perspective on life because they can no longer pretend that they are not disappointed and outraged.

Education comes from experience. It comes from encountering facts we have never met before or seeing them in a context which make other more familiar facts fit into a pattern that works. Realistic education begins with childish illusions and leads us down the road of facts to a more realistic understanding of ourselves and the world. Along the way we pay attention to our experience and change our mind when we need to.

PRIVILEGED PREMISES

But many times facts cannot dismiss illusions. We fight them all the way. We resist their presence. We abuse them by making them appear to be what they are not. We will not allow them to change our minds because we do not want to change our minds. We stare them in the face and still refuse what they have to say.

Ignorance is not the only cause of illusion. The second more painful cause is the refusal to accept what is emotionally unacceptable. We cling to our illusion because giving it up will hurt us or make us afraid. Our illusion becomes a privileged premise that always wins the argument.

Privileged premises are fairly easy to spot.

They are always immune to evidence.

The distraught mother sends her child to a school for gifted children because she believes that he is very smart. His school record has been dismal. He consistently gets low grades even though he is an obedient and compliant student. His mother has refused to accept this record as evidence that her child has mediocre intellectual ability and belongs in an educational environment that will be less traumatic and more supportive. She insists that the problem lies with incompetent and insensitive teachers who fail to understand the special needs and talents of her son. When the headmaster points out that almost all the other parents find the teachers to be exciting and wonderful she dismisses the evaluation by claiming that the other students are ordinary and that her son listens to "a different drummer." When her sister suggests that perhaps the young genius cannot perform because he has emotional problems, she subjects her son to endless hours of therapy and testing in order to dismiss the mental barrier that prevents his thoughts from emerging. At the same time, her daughter, who has displayed extraordinary achievement in both history, languages and mathematics is sent to public school, because, as her mother puts it, "Her success is all superficial. She lacks the depth my son has."

The devoted husband knows that his wife loves him. She refuses him sex and takes every opportunity to poke fun at his body. In public she mocks him and always arranges to sit next to somebody else. While she praises the achievements of all of her friends, she never acknowledges his skill as a business man and entrepreneur. The husband explains this behavior to others by pleading that his wife comes from a difficult home and an abusive childhood where no love or affection were ever expressed or manifested. It is hard for her to say what she really feels. All that he knows, and he can tell by looking into her eyes, is that she loves him very much.

The troubled clergyman is determined to confront the evil of the world without losing his faith. Unjustified pain and suffering are challenges to his beliefs but he is determined to proclaim the goodness of God. When a local drug addict dies from AIDS he is quick to point out that his death is a punishment for sin. Yet when his sister's infant child becomes HIV-positive through an infected blood transfusion, he announces that this infection is a way for God to test the faith of his family in ultimate divine justice. No matter what happens, both positive or negative, it always happens for the good. When his sister develops cancer and dies, he declares it to be a test of faith. When he discovers later on that she had committed adultery with her friend's husband, he declares the cancer to be a punishment for sin.

Privileged premises do not respond to facts. They never listen to them or open themselves to their reality. They are afraid of them. They want to hide them in boxes that do not fit or in grand theories that are not interested in them. With privileged premises the same evidence can prove that something is true or not true at the same time. The same evidence can prove your child is a genius even when it seems to demonstrate that your child is intellectually limited. It can prove your wife loves you even when it seems to demonstrate that your wife hates you. It can prove that the universe is a meaningful world even when it seems to point to the reality of a meaningless world. In the end, the facts are irrelevant. You will get to your conclusion no matter what the facts are.

Privileged premises love to announce themselves as "eternal truth." In the world of philosophy and religion they protect themselves with "forever and ever."

A young Michigan psychologist attended a mind shattering southern California retreat with a charismatic Indian guru. He returned to announce that he had learned the eternal truth about life. His spiritual experience was so overwhelming that he now knew, beyond a shadow of a doubt, that the material world was an illusion and that all human minds are simply imperfect parts of an all-encompassing divine mind. When it was suggested to him that maybe he was wrong, that maybe, in the euphoria of his personal experience, he was driven to exaggeration, he responded quite indignantly, "I know what I experienced. It was so powerful that I felt that I even transcended time. In one moment I was given the truth."

A television evangelist on a major interview program waved the Bible before the television camera and declared that "this book contains eternal truths that can never be refuted." The interviewer suggested that the most we can say about a statement or a book is that it *is* true. We cannot say that it *will* be true because some new piece of evidence might show up in the future to force us to change our minds. The fundamentalist looked him calmly in the eye and said, "You have obviously never been born again through faith, and through the grace of God. If you had, you would understand what I'm saying."

A North Korean Marxist philosopher announced at a Communist gathering in Pyongyang that Marx had laid bare the eternal patterns of history. The task of future intellectuals was to explain this truth and refine it. When a visiting American Marxist sociologist suggested that Marx had never made that kind of claim for his writing, the North Korean dismissed the "preposterous" statement with a warning that similar reservations had led to the downfall of Communism in the Soviet Union. He said, "Our commitment to the truth must be strong enough to cancel out all doubts."

"Eternal truth" has nothing to do with facts. Facts can only point to the truth. Facts can only yield tentative statements based on limited evidence. When facts are overpowering experiences and ecstatic encounters and mind blowing events, that is all they are—for all their *pizzazz*. They do not have the power to guarantee the future. They do not have the power to prevent some new fact from upsetting the apple cart. When you say that they do, you are entering the world of privileged premises. Religious dogmatists, political revolutionaries and mystic enthusiasts cross this line of limitation. And when they do they are no longer interested in the facts—only interested in defending the unbelievable. In a world of change and changing experience, finding an eternal truth is as likely as finding a square circle.

Privileged premises have a nasty side to them. When people who embrace them are driven to the wall by the facts, they become very afraid. They *need* to believe them. And they are not prepared to give them up. If the defenders are nice people and remain firmly calm, they will say, "You have not had my experience and therefore, you cannot appreciate what I am saying." They will privatize the facts, even though initially they tried to make a more universal appeal. "You can't possibly understand" is not a convincing argument even to the person who makes it. It is an act of desperation. It is a shutting out of all challenge because challenge is unwelcome. It is a way of saying, "No more facts, please."

When the defenders of privileged premises are nasty and afraid they become patronizing. They will often say, "I feel sorry for you. I feel sorry that you do not have the strength of my faith." Quite often they succeed in disarming their challengers. Many challengers take their pity to heart and come to feel sorry for themselves. "I wish I had his faith," "I wish I could believe the way he does." "I wish I had my own eternal truth." "I really admire people with that kind of conviction." All of these responses shift the burden to the challenger who now sees himself as some kind of defective processor of tentative truths. Living with doubt and uncertainty becomes a second-best alternative; at the most, a terrible alternative to the life of faith and eternal truth. People who should know better are now crying out for their own privileged premises. They confuse strong attachment with strength. They fail to see that clinging to privileged premises is a sign of fundamental weakness. Letting go is part of living with uncertainty. And being willing to live with uncertainty is the first sign of strength.

When the defenders of privileged premises are very nasty they turn to hate. Challengers become "infidels," "heretics," "apostates" and "suppressors." They are the enemy. Well-established organized religions have been very good at this procedure. Millions of people have been killed, expertly burnt at the stake and excommunicated because they challenged the privileged premises of the establishment. Unfortunately, some of the challengers are equally as dogmatic as their opponents. When they come to power, they inflict the same fanaticism on their enemies. They simply substitute one set of privileged premises for another.

Political revolutionaries have behaved no better than the religious dogmatists who persecuted them. The fascist and communist systems were built on privileged premises that weakened them and undermined their survival. They devoted too much time to defending the indefensible. The relentless pursuit of challengers was a reflection of their own internal doubts.

The persecuted turn into persecutors. From Scientology and the "Moonies" to Hare Krishna and Lyndon La Rouche, the purveyors of controversial ideas have turned their ideas into privileged premises. To protect their system against the facts, they withdraw from public display into there own little private world. All internal challenge is excluded. All internal challenge is punished. In such a closed world the irrational seems rational. And the transformation of a privileged premise into some higher wisdom or superior secret is what creating a cult is all about.

Even on the personal level privileged premises can breed hatred. Many a friendship has been destroyed because people have dared to challenge the sacred beliefs of their friends. They have suggested that a child is less than a genius or a parent less than a saint or a divorced partner less than a villain and have paid the price.

THE GRAND ILLUSION

The most powerful privileged premise of all is the *grand illusion.*

The *grand illusion* is the belief that we live in a meaningful world, that the universe enforces the moral agenda of human beings, that the fates conspire to reward the good and punish the wicked, that the behavior of men and women ought to reflect the behavior of destiny.

There is nothing in the daily experience of ordinary people to justify the grand illusion. All the happiness, joy, fulfillment, ecstasy and human satisfaction that exist cannot cancel out the pain, suffering, frustration and despair of the human condition. They go together, the good and the bad. No honest theory about life and the world can ignore the good. And no honest theory about the nature of reality can ignore the bad. The grand illusion does not say that the world is *sometimes* just. It says that it is *always* just. *Sometimes* is the equivalent of moral disorder, especially when we do not know when justice will strike.

But even if the grand illusion is not true, why dismiss it? It makes people feel good. It helps preserve law and order. Why leave people "naked" against the storm.

There is the rub. Strength comes from realism. And you cannot don the clothing of realism while still wearing the costume of illusion. They do not go together. They do not fit. You have to strip first before you dress for action. The style of realism is so radically different from the style of illusion—with all its apologies and with all its privileged premises—that you have to discard the old before you can attempt the new.

Dismissing the grand illusion is a necessary tearing down of the walls of resistance that prevent us from touching reality and making it work for us. Sanity comes from boldness not from timidity. The philosophic band-aid cannot be removed in shreds. It has to be ripped off.

We do not imagine that standing naked with the facts, without the confronting protection of old doctrines and old excuses, is easy. But staying sane is not easy. We do not discard the comforts of illusion without some tribute to the role they played and still play. Most people will not choose the path of realism because it is too different and too scary. They will either embrace the grand illusion with a special passion or linger in the limbo of believing and not believing at the same time. Others are the ambivalents who would like to choose the realistic path but are too frightened—or too cynical—to change direction.

Today the grand illusion provides many alternatives for those who wish to stay with it. If traditional religion is no longer satisfactory, there is new age spirituality. If new age spirituality is too exotic, there is still the dream of secular utopia. And if secular utopia has worn thin, there is the possibility of taking a little bit of each of the alternatives and making your own personal statement.

THE ALTERNATIVE

But if we are willing to dismiss the grand illusion, we have to come face to face with certain truths. These truths will serve as the foundation of our sanity.

There is no universal justice

We cannot expect to be rewarded for what we do well or punished for what we do badly. If nice things happen it is not because we are nice. If rotten things happen, it is not because we are rotten.

A student recently asked me what advantages flow from this harsh realistic outlook beyond simply the virtue of honest confrontation. I told him that I saw three in particular. The first was that lucky people no longer had the option of posing as virtuous people. So often in history "smug Calvinists" saw their success as a sign of divine favor and blessing. Luck is luck. In a crazy world a lot of silly undeserving people make it to the top of the greasy pole. Their success is no tribute to destiny.

The second advantage is that unlucky people do not have to feel guilty for their "suffering." The grand illusion is so powerful in the human psyche that despite all the previous attempts to tell unlucky people that their suffering is a mystery, many men and women feel that their misfortune is the result of their sins. They do not know *what* sin. But they are sure that there is one. And their agony is compounded by guilt. "What did I do wrong?," is a question we often hear, and sometimes ask. I remember the little five year old boy who lost his father in a freak accident, who asked me, crying, what he had done wrong that God had taken away his daddy. I told him that accidents happen, that he was not responsible and that he was strong enough to handle what could not be changed. He stopped crying.

The third advantage is that we do not have to spend endless time trying to prove that what is terrible is mysteriously wonderful. When my good friend lost half his doctoral dissertation in a campus fire in Ann Arbor, his pastor spent two hours explaining to him that in some mysterious way, not yet revealed, God intended to benefit his life. His parents told him that the suffering would make him a stronger person. His girlfriend said that God wanted him to spend another two years in Ann Arbor. Needless to say, some of this "insight" was very comforting. I told him that what had happened was a senseless tragedy and that what he had set out to accomplish was too important for him to surrender to blind fate and give up his ambition. He thanked me, for my honesty and concern. I was the first person to allow his tragedy to be a tragedy.

There is a liberating comfort in allowing things to be what they are and not to make them into what they are not. Losing a doctoral dissertation in a sudden fire is a terrible experience. It is not less terrible because it serves some mysterious divine agenda, or because it makes the loser stronger. There must be a thousand and one easier ways to make him stronger. Being allowed to acknowledge the pain and allowing others to acknowledge it is usually more comforting than theology.

Suffering has its own dignity. It needs to be recognized as suffering, not as some bizarre entrance to happiness. Realists are spared the necessity of struggling to whitewash reality.

There is no just and loving providence

God, if he exists, is the master of the universe. If he wants something to happen, it happens. If he wants something not to happen, it does not happen. Even human nature is his own creation. Some of what happens to human beings is "friendly." A lot of what happens is "not friendly." Nature is sometimes "loving." But it is also frequently "hostile." The "friendly" and "loving" parts are no more real than the "unfriendly" and "hostile" parts. If what you are looking for is a loving celestial parent, the evidence does not support the existence of such a God.

The options are clear. Either there is no God. Or there is an indifferent God. Or there is a hostile God. Or there is an incompetent God who tries to do good but does not have the power to do it. In the end, they all boil down to the same thing. Human beings have to rely on themselves for justice and love.

At a recent symposium of rabbis in which I participated, the meaning of the Holocaust was discussed. One rabbi acknowledged the horror, but said that he was emotionally unable to give up his belief in a just and loving God. Another rabbi felt that a divine purpose pervaded the tragedy and that the Holocaust had led to the establishment of the state of Israel and the fulfillment of a two thousand year old dream of the Jewish people. A third rabbi (a la Kaplan and Kushner) said that God tried to help but was powerless to prevent the tragedy. A fourth blamed the Holocaust on the Nazis and claimed that God was helpless to intervene since he had given the Nazis free will to choose their own behavior.

I found all these excuses to be silly, since a God you have to apologize for is already in trouble. I said that if God exists, there is no way for us to figure out his motivation. All you can confront is his behavior. And what we can learn from his behavior in the Holocaust is that human beings cannot rely on the kindness of the fates. Facts are facts. Six million innocent people died. And they died for no apparent good purpose. And, if there is a God, he did not choose to use *his* free will to rescue the victims from their enemies.

There is an enormous relief in not having to apologize for the facts. Black slavery was horrible. The massacres of Armenians were terrible. The extermination of the native Americans was a moral tragedy. The death of fifty million people in World War II was a travesty. These traumas served no useful purpose. If there is love, it is not built into the fabric of the universe. It is a human option, which many humans do not opt for.

Camus puts it bluntly: "A world that can be explained, even with bad reasons, is a familiar world. But in a universe divested of illusions and lights man feels an alien, a stranger. His exile is without remedy, since he is deprived of the memory of a lost home or the hope of a promised land. This divorce between man and his life, the actor and his setting, is properly the feeling of absurdity." (*The Myth of Sisyphus*)

Life and people are not at the center of the universe

Most mythology placed life, animals and people at the center of the world. Everything seemed to revolve around them, even the gods, even the stars. The earth and the heavens were the universe. And the earth took almost equal billing to the heavens.

But modern astronomy has given us a proper perspective on our place in the universe. Life is a fragile development in an air pocket on the surface of a small planet revolving around a minor star in a galaxy of trillions of stars, in a world of billions of galaxies. Although there has been much hope about the existence of other life on other planets in other star systems, none has yet been found. And, if found, it is highly unlikely it would bear any resemblance to the life that has evolved on this planet. We may imagine that, as in the movies, there are billions of English speaking humanoids passing through space and visiting our planet. But, despite all the reported sightings, they appear to be enormously shy.

Now certainly size does not determine importance. And if we are the only life around, that is no mean distinction. But, the reality is that our place in the universe is fairly limited. We may ultimately be able to escape our earthly air pocket. But escaping our solar system or escaping our galaxy, given the formidable challenges, of distance and time, seems less likely. Life is condemned to playing a much smaller part in the story of the universe than tradition has allotted it. If humans are important, it is because we are important to ourselves. And if life is important, it is because life is important to us.

The human agenda is not the same as the divine agenda. We are not gods. We are the children of the earth. Our fate is intertwined with our planetary air pocket and the life that shares it. And within that "small space" many competing agendas bump up against each other—species against species, group against group, individual against individual.

Only the human agenda is a moral agenda

We tend to see the universe as an extension of ourselves. The gods look like us and fill every corner of the world with our feelings and anxieties. We want to find love between the stars and justice in the behavior of the galaxies.

But stars and galaxies are not human. They do not have feelings. They do not have thoughts. Since they are inanimate they do not even have agendas. They simply exist without passion, without feeling, without communicating. They do what they do because they have to. They are driven by inner and outer forces of which they are unaware. They are victims of circumstance much more than we are.

We as humans do have feelings. We do have thoughts. We do have agendas. We are self-aware, filled with passion. Our lives are controlled by desire, dreams and aspirations. They produce the moral agenda. If we had no desires or passions, and if we did not share these desires and passions with other human beings, there would be no moral agenda.

The universe does not yearn for justice. But we do. The world is indifferent to our suffering. But we are not. The world does not care whether we live or die. But we care. The world cannot love. But we can. The universe derives no satisfaction from human pleasure and fulfillment. But we do. Realists know that the universe does not worry about us. We worry about the universe.

The first step of realism is to dismiss the *grand illusion*. It is to come face to face with the meaningless universe and say, "I am strong enough to live with you and with what you are. You are not always what I want you to be. You are not always what you ought to be. But I have to spend my life with you."

$$\boxed{7}$$

REJECTING DESPAIR
Step 2

ONCE YOU REJECT THE GRAND illusion, you are faced with two dangerous options. One is despair. The other is cynicism.

Despair begins with the complaint, "If the world is meaningless, then human existence is meaningless." If the world provides no guarantee of hope, then life is hopeless. Despair rests on the hidden premise that life's meaning comes primarily from outside of us. It is given to us by the fates, by destiny, by God. An absurd universe can only yield an absurd human story.

Arthur Schopenhauer, the German nineteenth century philosopher of despair, gave an angry voice to this complaint: "I cannot here withhold the statement that *optimism*, where it is not merely the thoughtless talk of those who harbor nothing but words under their shallow foreheads, seems to me to be not merely an absurd, but also a really *wicked* way of thinking, a bitter mockery of the unspeakable sufferings of mankind." (The *World as Will and Representation*)

Fifteen years ago I encountered one of the more extraordinary people to pass through my life. I was waiting in the airport in Los Angeles for my flight to Detroit. I was reading a newspaper and had placed my suitcase on the seat next to me. An Asian man approached me and asked me whether the seat beside me was available. I nodded while barely looking up and started to lift up my suitcase to remove it from the seat. The suitcase opened and all of my dirty laundry poured out on to the Asian's shoes. He laughed, bent down to pick up the embarrassing debris and helped me squeeze it back into the baggage. I thanked him. He started to talk. As I suspected, he was Vietnamese. He told me that he had fled Saigon in 1975, making his way to Bangkok and then to Los Angeles. He was Catholic, a graduate of the University of Paris. He had been a French teacher in Saigon for twelve years. Although he told me he was forty, he looked much older. He was either ill or had undergone some intense suffering. Suffering was the answer. His parents, who were wealthy landowners, had been arrested by the Vietnamese, and killed. His two brothers were sent to harsh re-education camps where they were savagely beaten. One died, the other was so brutalized that he was unable to speak and even now is confined to some hellish mental institution. He seemed reluctant to tell me his story, as though all this bad news was somehow in bad taste. But I could see that he really wanted to talk and that something far more terrible was waiting to be revealed. Tears filled his eyes as he went on with his story. He had come to America from Bangkok with his young wife. Speaking some English, he had become a French tutor for the children of a wealthy family in Beverly Hills. Six months before our encounter he took his family on their first vacation in America. He borrowed a friend's car and was driving north on the coastal highway to San Francisco when disaster struck. A speeding car failed to stay in its lane while rounding a curve and rammed his engine. His son was killed instantly. His wife lingered for four days unconscious in the hospital, before she died. He sustained fractures over his entire body and was now flying to New York to see a bone specialist about a femur that was not healing. As the man spoke, I could feel his pain. But I, strangely enough, did not sense despair.

Eager to console him, I said to him, "It is hard for me to imagine all the pain you must be experiencing. You have lost almost everything that you have loved. But I assume that your religious faith has sustained you through these terrible times."

The man smiled, hesitated, and then, with no apology, said, "Whatever faith I had is gone. The people I loved died before their time and with agonies they did not deserve. I no longer believe that there is a God I wish to talk to." "How then, are you coping with all this tragedy?" I asked. "You don't look defeated." He spoke without pausing to collect his thoughts. "I still want to live. I still want to have a family. I still want to be happy. No matter what has happened to me, I still want to go on." And, then, he reflected for a moment, and said, "I do not have any unrealistic hopes. I do not imagine that I can forget all the terrible things that have happened to me. I do not believe that the impossible pain in my heart will go away. I do not expect that whatever God is out there will console me and make everything alright. The world out there is no longer a place where I find any meaning. But I want to live and that gives meaning to my life."

I wanted to stay and listen to him but a loud voice announced my flight. I wished him well and said goodbye —and never forgot what he said to me.

The man had summed up what I had always felt and believed. The universe we live in is indeed, meaningless. For all its infinite complexity and vast dogmas, it has no agenda. It does not want to live or die. It does not want to love or hate. It does not want to help or harm. It has no desires. It just happens. There is force and motion. But there is no passion. Electrons and protons and neutrons stick together—not because they love each other—but because there is some dumb unconscious universal "glue" that holds them tight. Viruses invade cells and turn them cancerous—not because of malice—but because they have this dumb unconscious compulsion to duplicate themselves. The world is there; but it does not care whether it is there or not there.

But human beings do care. We want to live. We have desire. And desire breeds passion. We may be the universe's first audience. We turn the world into a drama of good and evil by what we want and need. Through our eyes we give the universe grandeur. Through our ears we transform motion into sound and music. Through our struggle to live we divide the world into the useful and the useless, the beautiful and the ugly, the wonderful and the terrible. The universe does not give meaning to human existence. It is human desire that gives meaning to the universe. We may be a microscopic audience in a microscopic auditorium. But without our applause, there is no play.

The world has no primary meaning. But the human will to live does. Even though we are part of the universe and have our root in the mindless atoms and molecules that move without wanting to move, our brains give us desire and purpose. More basic than Descartes', "I think, therefore I am" is the more passionate declaration. "I want, therefore I live." The purpose of human life comes from human need.

The world is neither our friend nor our foe. It is what we

bump into on our way to satisfying our needs. It is what other creatures bump into on the way to satisfying their needs. There are no
guarantees that we will get what we want. And there is no other stage
on which we can play out the drama of our life. The theater may be
less than what we want. There may be no grand director to insure our
success. We may feel the stage crowded with other people doing
their show and sharing the props. We may stumble and fall. We
may mumble and grumble. We may wail and protest. But the show
goes on because we are never quite sure how it will end.

Rejecting despair is no grand act of existential defiance. We do
not need the anger of resentment. "The world does not give a damn
whether I live or I die. But *I* do give a damn. Therefore, I will not surrender. I will not give the world the satisfaction of dying. I will do
what it refuses to do. I will affirm life. I will fight for life, even
though my struggle may be hopeless."

This dramatic defiance always seems to view the universe as
some kind of conscious adversary who desires our extinction. But there
is no one to stick your tongue out at. "I'll show you" is no more rational than "I worship you." Both presuppose a king that can respond to
either adoration or repudiation. Telling God off makes no more sense
than telling him that He is wonderful. It is like kicking the door. It
does not make any difference to the door.

The universe is neither our friend nor our enemy. Sometimes
it is warm and cuddly. Sometimes it is cold and hard. It is just there,
for us to use or not use, to touch or to avoid, to embrace or to flee
from. If it were all cold and all hard, the drama of life would not be
worth playing. Human life has meaning, first of all, because we
want to live and be happy. But if there is no chance for happiness, if
there is only the promise of pain and suffering, then there is not
enough meaning to persist in the struggle. If life is only a cruel

joke, where we want what we can never have, then suicide is more ratio-nal than survival.

Realists are romantic. But they never over-romanticize. They never turn the world into this polyanna paradise of *lovey-dovey* where even the lions and the lambs are kissing each other and everything turns out for the best. Nor do they dramatize life as a vale of tears filled with pain, agony and betrayal where love is a cruel deception and hope is the stuff of fantasy. Both extremes are illusions. Despair is often as unjustified as childlike faith. It is a poetic posture, charming in the young, but without any real substance.

Marilyn died in 1985. She was suffering from ovarian can-cer which had metastasized and had refused an experimen-tal chemotherapy because she did not want to endure "a use-less agony." Her death was a blow to her many friends, who were deeply attached to her. There was something about her that was very appealing and attractive. It was not always easy to explain why. She was short, stocky and a little chubby. Her nose was too long for her face and she spoke with a pronounced lisp that could have been turned by enemies, if she had any, into a comic routine. She was an outspoken lib-eral, often abusive, who was never reluctant to push her potential agenda. She was a traditional social worker, work-ing with inner city women on welfare cases and experi-encing the frustration of social problems she could not con-trol and people she could not help. When she was in her twenties she had a short, not too torrid love affair. When her partner left she was devastated, but she continued to search for another man to marry. She never found him and that disappointment was not easy for her because she wanted children of her own. What was appealing about her was her good humor, which helped to keep everything around her on an even keel. She was joyous but never ecstatic. She was sad but never depressed. She always poked fun at people who were into making a life style out of euphoria or gloom. Over-enthusiastic friends found that she calmed them down. Depressed clients found that she always insisted that they take advantage of opportunities they refused to notice. When she was forty she took up painting and became good enough to sell her paintings. Her art brought her deep satisfaction and eased the pain of her loneliness. She often described her paintings as her children. She saw them as part of her immortality and legacy. She continued to paint until the day before she died.

Marilyn and I were talking once about a mutual friend who had attended two EST (Erhard Seminar Training) weekends and had returned to announce that he was now "the master of his life." We laughed a little about the exaggeration. And then she noted, "If it only takes him two weekends to take charge of his life, it will only take him two weekends to lose it." She was right. He fell into the depths of doom and gloom shortly after his "victory" and stayed right there until he found the new salvation of Mind Control three weeks later. Life for him was always up and down. Fantasy euphoria was followed by fantasy despair. Needless to say, he was unendurable to his friends and helpless to take real control of his life.

Before Marilyn died, we spent an evening together. She became philosophic, "I want you to know," she said, "a lot of wonderful things have happened to me in my life and also a lot of awful things. But my life was always in balance because I never let the hard times make me forget the good times—and I never let the good times turn into "the message of the universe." I listened to her and told her how much I admired her for being so wise.

As Marilyn pointed out, the meaning of life does not come from the universe. It does not come from moments of ecstatic euphoria. It comes from the realistic hope that there is enough satisfaction around to balance out the painful frustrations of human existence. The real world cannot promise you a rose garden. But there are lots of flowers along the way.

BASIC TRUTHS

If you reject despair in a realistic way, then you recognize the following truths.

Disaster is not a primal statement from the universe

When bad things happen to us that we neither deserve nor can prevent, they are not making a personal statement. They are not punishments from on high. They are not malicious plots from wicked fates. They are simply "bad luck." They are the universe grinding away in its own impersonal fashion, indifferent to what it is doing and where it is going. We do not have to spend endless hours asking why. We can save ourselves the agony of soul searching and the bitterness of resentment. The laws of nature are blind, deaf and dumb. They cannot hear us if we holler at them, or ask them for explanations. They have no plan for us and they intend us no evil.

Some people find it hard to live with indifference. They would prefer that the universe was governed by a hostile parent or a hostile policemen than no parent or policeman at all. If they cannot be loved by God, they would prefer to be hated by the Devil than to be simply ignored. "Bad luck" is so impersonal. It leaves us unnoticed and insignificant. Sometimes children behave badly in order to attract the attention of their parents. But to have nobody you can defy is intolerable.

Realistic people welcome the indifference of the universe. Given all the painful surprises of life, it is a relief not to have to figure out *why me*. "That's the way the cookie crumbles," may sound flip, but it is really profound in a simple and honest way and saves a lot of time. So many people spend their time asking *why* when asking *why* is useless. They have no energy left over to cope with disaster.

Lyme Disease is a new development in the world of bacterial illnesses. An infected tick bites the innocent victim and produces inflamed joints, exhaustion and loss of memory. When Sarah came down with the painful disease, she was driven to despair by her endless *crying*. Why did she in the middle of a healthy and productive life, come down with this unwanted and undesired affliction? Why her and not someone else? What did it all mean? Her obsession to find answers led her to almost every clergyman and guru in town. All to no avail. They had no answers to satisfy her. Every recurrence stimulated a new flurry of philosophic inquiries. To no avail. To the pain of the physical illness was added the mental agony of her constant pursuit of the elusive answer. The depression that followed aggravated her condition. She was inconsolable and was unable to cope with the immediate demand of rearranging her life to deal with her disability. She became the perfect example of how fighting the facts does not provide happy illusions but only increases despair.

Realistic people do not ask *why* when *why* is inappropriate. They prefer to ask *how* questions. How do I cope? How do I confront this problem? How do I maximize my pleasure and minimize my pain? *How* people waste less time. They save their energy for important action. They resist despair by finding solutions—or making the best of what they cannot change.

There is no guaranteed harmony between my desires and the world

Realistic people are not surprised by frustration. They do not expect that the contours of their desires fit neatly into the contours of reality. They understand the competition. Other people have other agendas. Other living beings have other agendas. Inanimate objects have no agendas and just bump into whatever they bump into. There is no overreaching master coordinator to reconcile this confrontation of competing wants. If there was, it would add only one more agenda to the mess—his agenda.

Getting some of what we want is an amazing achievement in this disharmonious setting. From the distance, nature looks so peaceful, quiet and cooperative. Up close, where living creatures struggle for space and for food, it is more disturbing. Balanced environments, where intruders have not upset the delicate connection between species and species are really only balances of terror. Every group is "allowed" to eat just so much of another group. For the eater the arrangement is wonderful. For the eaten, there is little consolation in knowing that their death helps to maintain the balance.

Evolution is the story of disharmony—not only between life and life—but also between life and the physical universe. The human back is too new and too weak to handle standing up straight in a world of gravity. The human knee is too underdeveloped and too fragile to cope with the life style of walkers, runners and jumpers. The human brain is too big to permit infants to stay long enough in the womb to avoid helpless dependency. The romantic notion that everything in nature has its own comfortable niche is just plain false. Most mutations end up as failures. And most new life forms have long since perished. Natural selection is a relentless and cruel judge.

If you are realistic, a little disharmony does not depress you. You are always wonderfully surprised when desire finds its satisfaction. It is so hard making the match that missing the mark is no cause for wailing. If God is an "underachiever" then human beings need to be overachievers vigilant and alert to avoid the pitfalls of nature. Facing the facts may shatter false hope. But it also adjusts us to appropriate expectations.

Hope means flexibility

When I was a chaplain in Korea in 1957, I counseled a depressed dentist who had asked for an assignment in Germany and was shipped out to Asia instead. He was inconsolable. He felt abused and betrayed. He refused to leave his compound. He refused to socialize with fellow officers—or with anybody for that matter. His sulking was so aggressive that patients refused his service. He could only talk about how much he wanted to be in Germany and how he hated being in Korea.

I pointed out to him that whether he accepted it or not, he would remain in Korea for the next thirteen months. Getting to Germany was out of the question. He therefore, had two choices available to him. He could pine for something he could not have and go crazy or, he could embrace something he did have and learn to value it. I told him that I too had requested European duty and was rewarded with Korea instead. But I did not imagine that there was one and only one place I could be happy. In fact, I was intrigued by the opportunity of coming face to face with an Asian culture. And my curiosity had been rewarded by six months of new friends and star-tling revelations. If only he could see that his desires were far more flexible than his obsession would allow. The next day I took him to the home of a Korean friend. He had a thoroughly good time. He began to explore Seoul and the countryside on his own. Within six weeks he became very excited by the wonders of Oriental culture and was ecstatic over a weekend trip to the temples of southeast Korea. He had discovered that sometimes impossible environments yield their own satisfaction.

My social worker friend would have preferred a husband. But she discovered painting instead. My poet neighbor would have pre-ferred to be a published writer. But he became a much loved English teacher. My genius auto mechanic failed to be come a rich inventor. But he loves solving car problems that nobody else can handle. Second choices are not as good as first choices. But they are not all bad. Turn-ing life into either success or disaster eliminates all the wonderful in-between options that make life quite tolerable.

Meaning comes from perspective

Realistic people love peak experiences. But they do not depend on them for their philosophy of life. I feel so good and wonderful at the moment of ecstasy that I imagine that all of life, in fact, all of the uni-verse is exactly the way I feel at that moment. The danger is that peak experiences are often followed by "pits" experiences. The bottom falls out of our life. Everything fails. Hopelessness envelops us. We feel so miserable and so depressed at the moment of our failure that we imag-ine that all of life in fact, all of the world, is exactly the way we feel at the moment.

Intense experiences of either joy or hopelessness do not help us to find realistic meaning in life. They are too intense. They shut out the before and the after. They distort reality. They are incapable of giving credit to ordinary experiences of pleasure and pain.

So many people adjust their philosophy of life to the daily news. When the news is good they are optimistic. When the news is bad they are pessimistic. They never seem to take the time to balance the good news with the bad news. Political scandals turn all politicians into crooks. Urban race riots turn all race relations into failures. Feminist victories turn primary elections into harbingers of the feminist revolution.

I watch television evangelists with admiration and fear. They are such skillful manipulators of the peak experience. In the ecstatic fervor of the revival meeting everything seems possible, even the resurrection of the dead, even the sullen transformation of the human personality. Sick people are cured. Alcoholics throw away their bottles. Drug addicts turn to Christ. But, after the program is over, all of the "born again" go back to ordinary life. Many of them return to illness, alcohol and drugs. They cannot see beyond the moment. They are the victims of momentary enthusiasm and despair. Their lives are roller coasters of ecstatic commitments and dependent withdrawal.

Realistic meaning does not mean the guarantee of justice. It means the possibility of happiness. It does not mean ecstatic happiness. It means the opportunity to match pain with pleasure. The peaks and pits of life do not describe the journey. It is the road in between that counts.

CYNICISM

When you dismiss the *grand illusion*, the first dangerous response is despair, which must be rejected. The second dangerous response is cynicism.

Cynicism begins with the complaint, "If the world is meaningless, if there is no moral order built into the universe, if there is no guarantee that justice will prevail, if God is "dead" (as Nietzsche said) then there is no reason for me to be moral or ethical." Without the endorsement of God and the universe, there can be no valid ethics. Moral chaos reigns. All is permitted.

It has become very fashionable to blame immorality on lack of religion. The air waves are now filled with loud denunciation from fundamentalist preachers who accuse secular humanists of subverting traditional values. Even respectable intellectuals like Irving Kristol, Daniel Bell, Norman Podhoretz, and William Buckley insist that without religion, spirituality and some kind of divine authority, ethics is impossible. Believing in a meaningless world breeds cynicism. And cynicism breeds moral decay.

Although this argument is widespread in popular and intellectual circles, it is simply false. There is no evidence in history that societies which have been the most religious are less violent and more compassionate than more secular societies. Militant fundamentalists in the Muslim, Christian, Jewish or Hindu worlds thrive on hatred more than love. Of course, if you believe that holy war and the persecution of "non-believers" is the most important moral enterprise, then the fundamentalists win hands down. But therein lies the heart of the problem. What do you mean by *moral*?

If you mean by *moral*, the subordination of women to men, the primacy of motherhood as women's work, the reverence of parents by children, and the necessity of uniform public worship by the citizens of a nation, then, indeed, secularism has produced immorality. But if you mean by *moral* the freedom of individuals to choose their life style, the equality of the sexes, the toleration of ethnic groups and cultures which are different from your own, the pursuit of truth independent of dogma, the willingness to cooperate and share with strangers, then secularism has been responsible for more morality. There is no indication that the urban communities which are crime-ridden in America are less religious than the bourgeois communities where law and order prevail. The issue is income and class—not religion.

It is simply false to assert that religion and morality go together. Cynicism is inappropriate for people who dismiss the *grand illusion*. If you reject cynicism in a realistic way, you affirm the following truths.

Morality comes from the human condition

Ethics begins with the human condition. We are social beings hopelessly dependent on the help and nurture of other people. From the moment of our birth, from the moment we emerge from the womb as helpless infants, we know that we will not survive unless others enable us to survive. Human life is community life whether that community is a family, a clan, a tribe or a neighborhood. And communities work only if all members of the group believe that they are receiving as well as giving.

Natural selection has worked on the human species. For hundreds of thousands of years human beings who resisted community and fled cooperation were eliminated. They found no mates. They did not reproduce. Over a long period of time the people who survived developed a new emotion that reinforced their bond. We call it guilt. Guilt makes us serve our community even when we are not in the mood to. It makes us honor our parents, nurture our children, do our share of the work and offer our help to those who need it. Guilt and conscience go together. It would be naive to assume that they do not have some genetic basis.

Ethical rules do not fall from heaven. They do not exist in the outer reaches of outer space. They arise in the give and take of small communities struggling for survival.

Loyalty, love and sharing are the stuff of survival. In time, almost everywhere in the world, the conscience of loyalty and duty emerged, each culture adapting it to its physical context and social needs, but sharing with other cultures a core of commitments.

Later on, when the gods and religion entered the human belief system, old ethical rules were put into the mouths of the gods. The gods gave them added authority. The gods supported them with rewards and punishments. But they did not invent ethics. It is silly to imagine that people did not love and support their neighbors before Moses allegedly reminded them at Mt. Sinai. Religious ethics are not innovative. They are a reflection of moral standards that have evolved for centuries and have now become sacred. God endorses what the people have already decided is valid and workable. The divine voice is an echo of the human struggle.

The gods of every culture reflect the ethical style of that culture. Their moral authority does not derive from some divine right. It derives from the human experience and the human struggle that are the empirical support for what the gods command. First come communities. Then comes ethics. Then comes religion.

If we worship God today, we do not worship him because he is simply God. We worship him because he is good. And we can only know that he is good, if we have some standard independent of God to tell us what good means. That standard is the human experience.

And if we can no longer believe that he is good, if we can no longer believe that the world is a meaningful place, where justice wins out in the end, we still have the human experience and human memory and human guilt to give us morality.

Keeping promises is of no concern to most of the universe. It is only of concern to a limited number of creatures on the surface of the planet Earth, who have the power of speech and who know, from their very depths, that a community in which no person can trust the word of another, will die.

There are rewards other than heaven

Why be moral, if the good are punished and the wicked rewarded? Job asked that question. And so do the cynics. Guilt is never enough. Evolution has distributed it unevenly. Some feel it more intensely than others.

In a recent book called *The End of History: The Last Man*, Francis Fukuyama, a resident scholar at the Rand Corporation, explores the notion of progress and the future of liberal democracy. Along the way he identifies a human need long unnoticed by political philosophers, that explains the extraordinary success of democratic ideas in modern times. This need, he also points out, serves as the major reinforcement of morality.

It is the need for recognition. Human beings have an innate need to be affirmed by others, to be recognized as important, significant and useful. The greatest reward for moral believers is the recognition and approval of the community—whether that community is the establishment or a community of protest—or whether the approval is real or imagined. Many a lonely moral crusader is sustained by imagined approval.

Without communities approving our loyalty, courage and giving, the practice of morality is hard to sustain. Guilt itself may be nothing more than internalized disapproval. Anonymous urban conglomerates, which deteriorate into urban jungles, fail because they are anonymous, because they do not give approval and recognition, because they are not communities.

Given the evolution of humanity, the fear of hell is far less powerful in motivating morality than the admiring approval of leaders, friends and family. We are programmed to crave this recognition. Moral defectives are people who are born without this craving. They cannot be trained for ethical living. They are frightening sociopaths.

Emile Durkheim, the French father of modern sociology, rejected the religious foundation of morality. Responding to the German philosopher Immanuel Kant who insisted that God and ethics went together he declared: "Kant postulates God . . . We postulate a society specifically distinct from individuals, since, otherwise morality has no object and duty no roots." (*Sociology and Philosophy*)

When a "cynic" recently advocated to me that the masses needed to believe in divine reward and punishment (even though he did not personally believe in divine justice), otherwise they would cease to be ethical, I reminded him that *he* was very ethical. What was *his* motivation, if he did not believe? His motivation was the same as that of most people among the amorphous masses. Conscience and approval are a powerful combination.

Justice is a human enterprise

The universe may not be interested in justice. But *we* are. Unlike God we are neither omnipotent nor omniscient. We are very limited. But we do have power.

If there is to be justice in the world, only we can arrange for it. Nobody else is interested in the job. No one is calling for it from the depths of the universe. For cynics, justice is a waste of time because it cannot be guaranteed. For realists, justice is a worthwhile effort because it gives expression to their conscience. Making communities work is a noble labor.

When a student of mine volunteered to renovate houses in the inner city of Detroit, he ventured the opinion that his effort was only "a drop in the bucket," that it might make absolutely no difference in the end. I replied by telling him that I admired him for his decision, and that something has to be done to prevent our city from splitting in two, and that a renovated home was worth more than two thousand pious resolutions. He blushed at my approval, shrugged his shoulders and said, "We have to begin somewhere."

Realistic people are realistic—but they are not cynics.

Realistic people are realistic—but they refuse despair.

8

PURSUIT OF HAPPINESS
Step 3

IF YOU REJECT DESPAIR, THEN YOU admit the possibility of happiness. Choosing happiness is both realistic and rational. After all, what is the alternative—unhappiness?

Most people want to be happy. At least they say they do. And most people believe that they have a right to be happy, just as it says in the American Declaration of Independence.

Striving for happiness now seems to be such a normal goal. It is difficult to remember that, for most of human history, the pursuit of happiness made people feel guilty. Where life is hard, where people struggle for survival, the welfare of the group stands above personal satisfaction.

Duty was a much more appealing value than pleasure and still is for millions of people. A sense of duty was the glue that tied families, clans and tribes together. Where danger stalked the daily existence of peasant farmers, the pursuit of happiness seemed intolerably selfish. Duty and pleasure only came together when your community gave you strong approval for your gift of work and sacrifice. The pursuit of happiness ended up in the world of religion and was postponed to the afterlife.

But more affluent times brought happiness back to earth. Where food, clothing and shelter were more plentiful, pleasure and leisure could be valued without guilt. It was possible to think about happiness here on earth and not feel like sinners. In my childhood most adults were still into the culture of suffering. Life was defined by the unavoidable burden of duty and responsibility. Even if they were happy doing their duty, they would never admit it. Admitting pleasure would have diminished the moral quality of their behavior. If being ethical was pleasurable, how could it be ethical?

One of my aunts always got sick when she took a vacation. Having a good time was not her idea of the good life. Pain was a moral relief. It was natural and never had to be defended. But pleasure always had to be explained and defended. It was dangerous to be happy. Destiny always waited for you to smile. When you did, it blessed you with disaster. It was simply safer to pretend to be miserable. If you looked pitiable enough, nothing worse would happen.

Today most of us no longer share this discomfort. Some of us are so absorbed in the "pursuit of personal happiness" that moral issues rarely intrude. Others are convinced that their search for happiness is perfectly compatible with an ethical approach to life. Still others believe that individual fulfillment is what morality is all about.

In the last two centuries many philosophers have given happiness moral status. Thomas Jefferson declared it a right. John Stuart Mill glorified "the greatest happiness of the greatest number." George Santayana made happiness the reasonable goal of life. And Bertrand Russell devoted a whole book to the "conquest of happiness."

But what *is* happiness?

NATURE OF HAPPINESS

There may be as many definitions of happiness as there are people seeking it. After all, being happy is not a physical thing like having a nose or being six feet tall. It is tied to feelings which are not easily observed and which change all the time.

One colleague of mine maintains that happiness is simply indefinable. It is as primary as the color red, he says, and can only be discerned by the inner eye of the person experiencing it. When you are happy you are happy, and that's that. Discussions about what happiness is are a waste of time. It can only be apprehended by some internal pointing finger.

Another colleague, a philosophy professor, dismisses that approach as no answer looking like an answer. Happiness, he asserts is directly related to human desires. When our desires are frustrated we are unhappy. When they are satisfied we are happy. Happiness is a matter of degree. The more desires satisfied the happier we are.

Both answers have problems. The first is so subjective that two people with radically different experiences can both claim the same label. The second is on the right track but it does not distinguish between very important desires and less important desires. Millions of people are willing to confront pain and frustration in order to achieve important goals. They are willing to deny one need in order to satisfy another need they regard as more significant. They are willing to postpone one satisfaction now in order to realize more fulfilling satisfactions later on. A lot of happiness is in the anticipation of results. Conscientious parents and hard-working students know that.

Perhaps the best way to deal with the issue of happiness is to identify its "symptoms." What are the internal and external signs of being a happy person?

At least three "symptoms" seem obvious.

The first is pleasure. We do not have to be hedonists to understand the pleasure of pleasure. Some pain is unavoidable in the happy life. Even suffering plays a minor role. But avoiding pleasure and cultivating pain is masochism, not happiness.

The second is the sense of being in control of your life. Believing that our fate and destiny are in the hands of powers we neither know nor understand can make us both nervous and unhappy. Happy people feel that they can direct the course of their own lives and get where they are going, even though the going may be rough.

The third is having few regrets. People who are obsessed with their mistakes, who are stuck on the missed opportunities of the past, have no time to be happy. People who suffer bad luck and who are tied to the treadmill of asking *why*, also have no chance to be happy. The past is unchangeable. And trying to change it is the source of most unhappiness.

By studying these three "symptoms" in greater detail we will have a better idea of what happiness is and how to achieve it.

PLEASURE

Traditional ethics is generally ambivalent about pleasure. On the one hand it recognizes that ethical behavior often requires painful discipline and painful sacrifice. But, on the other hand, it is reluctant to recommend a life of unceasing pain.

There are two ways in which the tradition handles this ambivalence. The most popular way is to promise pleasure after death. A lot of pain now may mean a lot of heaven later. A lot of pleasure now may mean an eternity of hell in the world to come. But many people today are no longer so confident that this promise is reliable. They suspect, quite justifiably that it is part of a grand illusion. Or they are not quite sure that the pleasures that are promised are the pleasures they want.

I was recently accosted by an evangelist who warned me about the dangers of hell and the opportunities of heaven. I asked him for more information about heaven. What exactly is the program of activity? What do disembodied spirits do all day that is so exciting and so compelling that I would want to sign up for eternity? He was taken aback by this pragmatic consumer culture approach to the afterlife. He mumbled something about peace and quiet, ethereal music and the endless contemplation of the Divine Presence. I told him that I thought that the program was boring and that I was not interested. He became flustered. He had never imagined that the problem with heaven was not that it was unbelievable but that it was unattractive. For human beings accustomed to bodies, the "activity" did not sound like a lot of fun. Even a peak experience, sentenced to eternity, can lose its luster.

The second way that the tradition copes with its ambivalence to pleasure is to declare that pain is really pleasure in disguise. This approach may be called the "suffering is good for you" school.

The business failure has the opportunity to enjoy the beauties of nature and the love of his family. The handicapped veteran is able to discover the latent artistic talent he never knew existed. The traumatized widow learns that she is now free to do all the things she could not do before. Bad things turn out to be really good things. Pain turns out to be the prelude to pleasure.

The most striking example of this approach is the "how lucky I am" sequence. I was recently in the hospital to see a friend who was the innocent victim of a traffic accident. Both his legs, his right arm and his nose were broken. When I walked into his room he was a vision of helplessness, bandaged and casted and dangling from pulleys. Although he looked depressed he spoke euphorically. He said to me, with all honesty, "I was really lucky. I could have been killed." And I thought to myself, "If this is luck, then what is a catastrophe?"

But, of course, I was being too realistic, I had failed to tune into the creative possibilities of denial. The "how lucky I am" proponents turn pain into pleasure simply by comparison. Every pain becomes less painful, even pleasurable, when compared to the worse horror that might have happened. All we have to do to feel good is to imagine some greater disaster and then feel grateful that it did not occur. Pleasure by comparison is an effortless tactic that makes us "lucky." It never occurs to the defenders of luck to compare what has happened to something better, like not having any accident at all. If any disaster can become a success by reverse invidious comparison, then there are no real disasters. All pain becomes pleasure. And all distinctions between the two fade into the world of Pollyanna.

Pleasure has no meaning if pain does not. Truly happy people can endure pain because they have experienced enough pleasure to compensate for it. They do not have to pretend that pain is not pain, that suffering is not suffering, that tragedies are not tragic. It may be the case that some suffering is therapeutic, that we learn to avoid worse suffering because of our experience, or that we grow stronger in the face of adversity. But most pain is just rotten, whether it is physical or emotional. Pleasure cannot be pleasure if it is the same thing as pain.

There are three kinds of pleasure: sensual, emotional and intellectual. Most gratifying experiences combine all three. Sensual pleasure, by itself, is too fleeting to be significant. After it departs it often makes us feel empty like promiscuous sex and compulsive eating. Emotional pleasure, by itself, is too immediate to be comfortable. Like love and wonder it needs to be related to the goals we choose for our lives. Intellectual pleasure comes from seeing the order of things. Pieces of our experience fit into some greater whole that gives them meaning. But alone, by itself, intellectual pleasure is too ethereal. It needs to be grounded in earthier passions.

A philosophy teacher found that listening to well performed Mozart was an ultimate experience for him. The beauty of the sound, the intensity of the feeling, the awareness of the musical patterns, all added up to an exquisite pleasure.

A new bridegroom touted the pleasure of his new marriage. The physical passion, the feeling of deep attachment mutually shared, and the sense that this commitment fit so perfectly into what he wanted out of life, all combined to give him an experience of lasting satisfaction.

A successful criminal lawyer sang the praises of his work. He enjoyed the physical presence of the courtroom audience. He was turned on by the excitement of confrontation. He was stimulated by the opportunity to make a convincing story out of chaotic evidence.

Most pleasures that count, for both the educated and the uneducated, are far more complex than the simple sensual stereotype that traditional opponents love to use. If hedonists are people who value and pursue pleasure, realistic hedonists never settle for simple one-dimensional pleasure. In fact, the most profound pleasures arise out of the problem-solving daily routine of the human condition. Some of them even involve the risk of pain.

Achievement in the face of danger excites us. How else do you explain the human addiction to games? We invent problems in order to solve them. We scare ourselves with defeat in order to taste the pleasure of victory. Men and women are invariably game-players. That is why heaven is so colossally boring, a place with no real pleasure. Eternal peace and forever and ever contentment are humanly unendurable. Only devilish rebellion would make it tolerable.

There is an important distinction between passive and active pleasures. Passive pleasures involve no risk of pain and anxiety. They are attached to environments where there are no conflicts and no dangers. They prefer the imagined safety of the womb, where babies float in mindless security. People who chase passive pleasures use words like "harmony," "bliss" and "surrender" a lot. They want a place where they can feel safe, feel loved, and feel dependent with no risk of subversion. They want a place which has nothing at all to do with the human condition.

Philip was a successful stockbroker who decided to retire early at 58. He was continually complaining about the "rat race" of business, the "jungle of competing" in the stock market and the sleazy business tactics of his competitors. He wanted *out*. He wanted peace and quiet. He wanted, as he put it, the bliss of having no responsibilities. His children had grown up and left home. His retirement pension was more than adequate. He moved to Arizona where "nature was next to perfect." But paradise turned to hell. Problems and responsibilities did not disappear. His wife developed a back problem. Two of his three children divorced and wanted to move to Arizona to be near him. Golf was a part-time challenge, but not a very meaningful one. Sunny days depressed him because they promised happiness and he felt *lousy*. Despite his mumbling and grumbling, the main source of his pleasure had been his work, and that was gone. There were no significant challenges and risks. Only routine family problems and illness. Life became an endless trip of sun and nothing, and worries that would not go away. The excitement of winning for big stakes in a big game had gone away. He was consigned to the bliss of *blah*.

Life without problems is a utopian fantasy. It is divorced from the human condition. We are the evolutionary children of hunters struggling to survive. There is no place we can run to, even in retirement, where there are no problems. Sometimes big challenges are more pleasurable than small routine challenges. They promise more intense satisfaction, if we can overcome them. A life of eternal bliss and safety is the life of a zombie. It has nothing to do with human happiness. The meaningful life is not to get rid of problems. It is to live with them, confront them and sometimes win.

Active pleasures find their context in the world of relentless challenges. We cannot rely on the kindness of the fates. There are all these surprises, both pleasant and unpleasant, which invade our lives and never stop coming. Confronting problems, with all its risk of success and failure is the source of human happiness. When we win we feel the pleasure of achievement. When we lose we feel the pain of failure. The greatest pleasures always involve the greatest risk.

When Larry was growing up in the inner city of Detroit, he made some very important decisions. His family owned a bakery, and they were willing to give it to him, if he would start working full-time after he graduated from high school. He had a girlfriend who wanted to get married and have children. Everything seemed to be falling into place for a safe and secure existence. But he wanted to be a physician. His family balked at the idea of his going to college. No one in their community had ever gone beyond high school. His grades in the sciences were only average. He had a hard time concentrating on his studies. But he was determined. He gave up the bakery and his girlfriend. He found nighttime employment in the factories. He rarely slept, because his studies consumed most of his free time. His overwhelming worry was that he would commit himself to four years of hard work and devastating anxiety and never get admitted to medical school. The stress became almost unbearable. There was so much discipline and pain to the uphill battle. Yet he persevered. He trained himself to concentrate. He hired tutors for sciences. He avoided unnecessary social entanglements. And he made it. He was admitted to the University of Michigan Medical School. He had confronted an overwhelming problem and had won. The victory was not easy. There was always the gnawing fear that he would not be able to master the next step. But the acceptance gave him the "happiest day of my life." Of course, it could have been the "gloomiest day of my life," if he had failed. Therein lies the irony of happiness.

Lives that avoid confronting challenges, that always seek safety and security, peace and quiet, may provide moderate pleasures, but they never provide the grand pleasures. Happiness may not even be good for your health. The most fulfilled people often experience enormous amounts of stress. Heavenly bliss may be a trap for mediocrity. Life is a balancing act. If I am too concerned with staying safe, I may end up with a long and boring life. But if I jump to the excitement of every risk, my life may be too short to savor any long-run pleasure.

One of the deepest pleasures of all is the sense that we are not completely safe, that we are not in the hands of some benign providence which will provide for all our needs, that our lives are ours to mold and fashion according to our own will. In a world of continuous problems it is more satisfying to experience that we are more and more in control of our lives, than to rely on promises of safety that cannot be kept.

"Nothing so saps the profound resources of life as finding life too easy," declares the Spanish philosopher Ortega y Gassett.

SENSE OF CONTROL

Feeling the masters of our lives is no easy achievement. As small specks in an infinite universe, we have good reason to think ourselves insignificant, to imagine ourselves helpless pawns of forces we do not control.

Traditional religion has reinforced this feeling of powerlessness. The world is orderly. But we are too limited to understand the order. Whatever happens, happens for the best, even though we have no idea what the "best" is. In the face of all this mystery, the only decent option available to us is resignation. The sign of resignation is worship. And the meaning of worship is our total dependence on forces we can barely comprehend. We even offer thanks for gifts we are not quite sure we have received.

On the surface this dependence seems comforting. After all, children are happy who are dependent on their parents and who are not fully aware of why their parents choose to do what they do. As long as there is faith and trust, ignorance can be bliss. Being responsible for our lives can be a heavy burden. God may be doing us a favor by relieving us of the load.

But dependence can also mean fear and anger. We are afraid of a future we do not control. We are angry at waiting for what never seems to come. Although, in religious settings, we are reluctant to express our fear and mask it with protests of gratitude, it lingers beneath the surface and is redirected. We come to fear and hate our "enemies," the people who challenge our faith. And the more we are uncomfortable with our dependence, the more we claim to love it.

Being a child is nice for children. But, in the end, it is depressing for adults. It is humiliating to be the pawn in somebody else's game. It is demeaning to be the actor in somebody else's play. We can never be fully independent. Yet we have a need to be separated from the intense togetherness of infancy.

Our long childhood (longer than for other fellow creatures) makes us ambivalent about responsibility. We have learned the skills of dependence so well that we tend to use them even when they do not give us much satisfaction. Most people prefer the familiar pain to the unfamiliar pleasure. We like to do what we know how to do best. And being a child is the first "profession" for which we train.

It is difficult to take control of our lives. Naive expectations from childhood linger in our minds, even when we grow up. We imagine the world to be what our infant mind conceived.

One of the new projects in life, that has become the rage over the past thirty years, is "finding yourself." Young people, by the bourgeois thousands, drop out of school and travel the globe in search of themselves. Countless numbers of "menopausal" men and women leave their spouses and begin a frantic hunt for the "real me." Ambivalent men and women actively avoid any commitment to either work or people while bemoaning their inability to get in touch with who they are.

On the surface, the project of finding yourself does seem a bit odd. After all, if we do not know who we are or where we are, who does? But, perhaps, the search has to do with the fact that so much of what we think and feel is in the unconscious part of our mind and we are unaware of it. Or, perhaps, it has to do with the fact that we often need space and time to develop a perspective on our lives.

I do not think so. If that were the case, both psychotherapy and experience would cure the anxiety. The issue is philosophic. The problem is a childlike view of the universe.

If I am a child, I know that I have an assignment. Parents give me assignments. Teachers give me assignments. Why not God and the universe? If I have an assignment I do not have to be responsible for my life. I do not have to choose among options. I simply do what I am supposed to do. The burden of autonomy is lifted from my shoulders.

"Finding yourself" is an avoidance activity. Self-insight will not help. It will simply reveal that we like and want many things, all of which we cannot have. Perspective will not help. It will only disclose that there are many things we do well, all of which we do not possess the time or the energy to do. Time will not help. It will only postpone decisions we should have made a long time ago.

Cults, religions, sects and revolutionary political movements are popular because they give you an assignment. They relieve you of unpleasant responsibility. They also give you dependence and the guilt of feeling resentful.

Long-run happiness is opposed to assignments. It does not

wait for the universe to tell us what to do. It does not expect clear messages from destiny. It knows that the answer is not found. *It is chosen.* Choices, no matter how well informed, are still choices. And no choice is ever completely right. Every decision has both advantages and disadvantages. We weigh the consequences of each alternative and then plunge in. Happy people do not postpone decisions indefinitely. They know that no matter how long they wait or how long they search, they still have to "plunge." They do not "find" themselves. They design themselves.

A student of mine recently took a series of aptitude tests. He discovered, to his chagrin, that his skills and temperament would make him both a good physician and a good lawyer. This discovery filled him with anxiety. He would have preferred to be qualified for only one profession. Destiny had been too generous. He soon faced the prospect of making the choice. He handled his anxiety by dropping out of school. As you guessed, he is presently in the process of "finding" himself.

People who prefer to remain in the limbo of indecision find neither the pleasure of self-control nor happiness. The search for "my assignment" is a futile one. But making decisions is hard for many people. They want to avoid the risk of responsibility. If they cannot find their assignment, they will at least bask in the safety of everybody's approval. Needing everybody's approval runs neck and neck with "finding yourself" as a sure path to unhappiness.

Most people hate hostility and confrontation. Some people are so terrified by anger that they will do almost anything to appease their judges. They want to find a way for everyone to love them. The more they try to please the more they lose control of their lives. In time desperation sets in. By pleasing one person they offend another. by rushing to win the approval of this friend, they lose the approval of that friend. There are too many authorities. And the bosses all disagree.

Pitiful people respond to this impasse by self-demeaning behavior. They become so careful and innocuous that their will is paralyzed. Or they deny the rejection they are experiencing and pretend that hate is love. Or, worst of all, they become peevish and rebellious, make an emotional flip-flop and then claim that they do not need anybody's approval.

Sylvia adopted all three "loser" tactics. A dutiful child, who always did what her mother told her to do, she married a demanding husband who was dominated by his own willful mother. Neither her mother nor her husband, nor her mother-in-law could agree on anything. With three quarreling bosses she lost whatever shred of control she had over her own life. Finding it impossible to win everybody's approval, she turned to denial. She would pretend that the disagreements were trivial and that the continuous scolding was really an act of love. Finally, one day, unable to tolerate her failure to please everybody, and worn down by continuous appeasement and rejection, she exploded. From that moment on she became aggressively defiant, telling anybody who would listen that she "didn't give a damn" whether anybody liked what she did. She was the master of her life and that's all that counted. Within two months she had alienated all of her friends, even those who had sympathized with her plight.

While it is true that we do not need everybody's approval in order to be happy, it is also true that we need some approval. Without the respect of the people we respect we can have no self-esteem.

And without self-esteem, we do not have the emotional power to take charge of our life. The path to happiness and self-control is certainly not to try to please everybody. But it certainly is not the refusal to please anybody. We need to be subjective. Only the people we respect can be our judges. Successful people limit the number of trials where they play the defendant. But they do not dismiss all trials.

We are dependent on the goodwill and approval of caring parents, friends and co-workers. We also need the approval of expert strangers whose competence we value. But the hostility of others is the test of our character and self-control. We are not masochists. We do not waste our energies on trying to get what we do not need. If we try to make decisions with everybody's approval we will fail. If we try to make them with nobody's approval, we shall lose our self-respect. Happiness lies somewhere in between.

Taking control of your life needs one more caution. Know your limitations as well as your talents.

In recent years, in response to the traditional message that people are weak, powerless and sinful, the new psychology has sought to make people feel better about themselves. Quite appropriately, we are told that we have much more power than we think we have, or that we have much more talent than we give ourselves credit for. Knowing and using our own power and talent are important to our happiness.

But knowing our limitations is equally important. Pretense is just as dangerous to our welfare as is low self-esteem. We can be undone as much by overweening ambition as by timidity. If we aim for what we cannot achieve our illusions will prevent us from ever taking control of our lives.

The happiest people I know are the men and women who have

a realistic view of their talents and then proceed to develop them. The most unhappy people I know are the men and women who let their desires become a substitute for their abilities and who chase what they cannot capture.

> Tom wanted to make a career out of acting. He was encouraged by his success as the lead in his high school play and was determined to go to Broadway. His parents and teachers, who were skeptical of his dramatic talents, were reluctant to restrain him because they felt guilty and awkward telling him how to lead his life. So, of course, he went to New York and ended up becoming a successful waiter and an unemployed and depressed actor. He continually complained about "bad luck" and "the system." But he had clearly overestimated his talents. He lacked the special charisma that makes the difference. His cousin, who was equally interested in dramatics, but who was far more realistic about his non-charismatic style chose law. His dramatic abilities were an asset to his legal work. He is now a "star" in a local courtroom while his more "ambitious" relative is a Broadway failure.

Trying and taking risks and making high demands on your talents are important for happiness. But they are not enough.

Drive and ambition are not the most important factors in becoming the master of your life. Realistic, self-awareness comes first. Striving for attainable goals is the foundation of self satisfaction. Being a "big fish in a little pond" is certainly preferable to being a dead fish in a big sea.

Since we live in a world where everything is inflated, money and political promises especially, it is no mystery why ambition is "inflated." Many people have difficulty taking control of their lives because they have inappropriate expectations. They expect work without tedium, love without responsibility and success without limitations.

Competence is a better guarantee for self-mastery than therapeutic cliches. Too many people strive to be unique and original when they would be far more successful being ordinary. A good accountant is better than a bad poet. And a good parent is superior to a mantra missionary. We all know the story of the ugly duckling who turned into a swan. But most ducks are not swans. And, if they try to be, they cannot remain ducks. Ambition is part of hope. But it needs to be good-humored.

Taking control of our lives demands realism. It is a balancing act between the timid refusal to take risks and fantasies of omnipotence. If we are willing to take responsibility for our lives, if we refuse to seek the approval of everybody, and if we especially let our talents speak for themselves, we have a pretty good chance of achieving enough self-mastery for happiness.

FEW REGRETS

Clearly the unhappiest people I know are the people who spend their time reliving the mistakes of the past. Regretting the past takes up enormous chunks of human conversation. Only trying to figure out who is to blame is more time consuming.

For some people the errors of the past are obsessions that torture them daily. Events that took place many years ago remain as fresh as they were in the moment of their happening. Sometimes time and memory exaggerate the details and turn trivial events into full-fledged horror stories.

People who live regretfully in the past have very little opportunity for happiness. They are engaged in a project they can never succeed at. What they really want to do is to change the past, to make it different, to go back and start all over again. But the past is unchangeable, as immune to human or divine intervention as the karma of the Hindus. What was, cannot be altered.

But determined "regretniks" are not deterred by the obvious. Their ritual continues because they cannot give up their fantasy. To do so would compel them to accept the unacceptable and to come face to face with the limitations of the human condition.

Laura is a divorcee who, in the enthusiasm of the feminist revolution, dismissed her husband and gave up the custody of her children. Although euphoric at first, her enthusiasm vanished when she was confronted with the reality of her options. Middle-aged and unattractive, endowed with a teacher's certificate at a time when nobody needed teachers, she quickly discovered that she was lonely and poor and rejected by her own children. She recovered enough to become a real estate agent. But she had no real energy for work or for finding lovers and friends. She spent most of her time moaning about the mistake she had made. "Why did I do it?" She kept asking. Nobody had an answer to satisfy her. After a while, even her old friends abandoned her. They were alienated by her obsession. She was paralyzed by regret.

Sam is a young lawyer who is unable to focus on his work. Ten years ago, after graduating from law school, he turned down an offer to join a major legal firm in order to go into business with his father. The choice to work with his father was a mistake. Their personalities and values were incompatible. The recession undermined their markets. And aggressive unions ate up their profits. The business collapsed. He was estranged from his father. Offers from major law firms were no longer available. He was starting up his own law office. But he was unable to concentrate on his work. The "stupidity" of the choice he had made ten years before made him angry and sad. He kept wishing that he had the option to go back in time and set things right. He kept asking people what he should do.

We all make mistakes, some trivial, some serious. We all have regrets. We all confront the unchangeable past. But some people who make mistakes are happy. And some like Laura and Sam, are desperately unhappy. The happy ones know when to try resignation.

Resignation is a strange emotion. It is a special form of apathy. Normally, it is harmful. It makes people passive when they should be active. It makes them docile when they should be angry. But sometimes it is useful, even positively beneficial. Sometimes, ironically, it activates people and rescues them from depression.

Accepting the immutability of the past is an act of resignation. It is the recognition that nothing we do or say will make one change in what has already happened. It is the good humor to admit that regret is a waste of time. Only the future can be affected by our anxiety and work.

Of course, dismissing the past does not mean that we do not learn from the past. "Those who do not remember the past are condemned to repeat it," said philosopher George Santayana. Hopefully, we will not repeat the mistakes we have made. But dismissing the past is dismissing the irrational fantasy that we can change it.

The happiest people I know make many mistakes. They sometimes arrange foolish divorces. They sometimes choose hopeless careers. They sometimes undermine treasured friendships. But they do not linger in the past. They are experts at using resignation where resignation is appropriate. If they have energy to spare, they devote it to the future.

REALISTIC HAPPINESS

Happiness, in the abstract, is pleasure without pain. Realistic happiness is a life in which pain is inevitable, but in which pleasure outweighs the pain. It is a life where problems never cease, challenges never disappear, choices never go away and mistakes can never be repealed. Pursuing realistic happiness means staying in this messy world and struggling for victories until the day of your death.

9

APPROPRIATE EXPECTATIONS
Step 4

W HEN I WAS A CHILD IN ELE-
mentary school, in the third grade, I made friends with the most popular girl in my class. She was pretty and smart and very selective about
choosing her friends. I was very proud to be her friend. Every time she
greeted me or spoke to me I felt that I was her special friend, even
though she never said so and even though she spent most of her time
with others. When I turned nine I invited her to my birthday party.
But she never showed up. I was crushed, yet wanted to believe her when
she told me that she was sick. Three weeks later she celebrated her
birthday. Many kids from the class were invited. I was not. I felt so

humiliated. I did not know at the time that I was suffering from inappropriate expectations.

When I took my first trip to France over thirty years ago, I was filled with high excitement. I imagined that the people of Paris were warm and fun-loving and that they would embrace me, a stranger, with a welcome given to friends. I saw myself sitting on the edge of the Seine sipping wine and basking in all the friendliness and courtesy that would come my way. But I was in for a rude surprise. Most of the people I encountered were self-absorbed, indifferent and rude, just like most of the people back home in big city America. They were bored with tourists and a little hostile to their continuous intrusion and demands. Shopkeepers saw nothing special in me. The "famous" Left Bank cafes were filled with tourists staring at tourists. The traffic was relentless. Not even the architectural wonders of the physical Paris could restrain my disappointment. Of course, I was suffering from inappropriate expectations.

Most unhappiness in the world stems from painful and dreadful events. But much unhappiness comes from experiencing positive things, but never being able to see them as positive because we expected them to be so much more. So many of us live in a world of perpetual disappointment and sadness which we have designed with our own exaggerated hopes.

HOPE

Anticipation is as important as reality. For human beings life is more than the present and the memories of the past. It is also the vision of the future that motivates our action.

Foresight is a human survival skill. In a world filled with

danger our big brain enables us to anticipate peril. Sometimes it uses intuition. Sometimes it uses reason. Present clues help us understand future consequences.

Some people look into the future and see only doom and failure. They are understandably unhappy. Others look ahead and see events that are exciting and wonderful. They are generally happy. Without hope happiness is meaningless.

Optimists are not necessarily people who have led easy lives. Nor are pessimists people who have experienced many adversities. On the contrary, some of the most coddled men and women I know are pessimists. And some of the most harried are optimists. Past experience is not the determining factor. The style of personal expectations is.

Pessimists generally have high expectations for the universe and other people. They expect other people to be noble, kind, generous and responsible. They expect the universe to be concerned with their moral agenda. They expect the world to be fair. And, of course, they are always disappointed. No matter what marvelously positive events may occur, it is never enough.

> Paul is a pessimist. He is appalled by all the violence in the world. He is depressed by all the bigotry and hatred in America. He has trouble living with the injustice of the universe. When Robert Kennedy and Martin Luther King, Jr. were assassinated twenty-seven years ago, he became a confirmed cynic and retired to his private world of music and reading. He makes no plans for the future because, despite the end of the Cold War, he anticipates a nuclear holocaust. Given his expectations, life has been for him a continuous disappointment.

Sally, is an optimist. Although she has a hard job as a social worker in the inner city, she is amazingly resilient. The inner city people she works with are flaky and ungrateful. The politicians she lobbies are corrupt. Her personal life was the host to a painful tragedy, the accidental death of her son. Even though she repudiated the utopian politics of her fellow students in the sixties, she remains consistently hopeful. Her utopian friends have turned into cynics.

The difference between Sally and Paul lies in the nature of their expectations. She has very low expectations of other people. She believes that most people, including herself, are self-absorbed, caught up in their own agendas. She believes that most people have difficulty empathizing with the needs of others, especially strangers, for any length of time. She believes that most social institutions resist change and need to be assaulted many times before they are open to alteration. She believes that the universe does not give a *damn* about the moral agenda of human beings and is generally "unfair." If the good suffer and the wicked prosper she is not surprised. Her expectations allow her to notice the positive things that happen in the world. She is always amazed that, given all the change of the past two hundred years, there is as much law and order, peace and stability, presently on our planet. In short, she is a realist about the human condition. And, being a realist, she has every reason to be an optimist.

Men and women, with appropriate expectations of life, are maintaining marriages, sustaining friendships, assuming useful work and supporting the slow, gradual achievement of world peace. They are the optimists of humanity. And they are the candidates for sanity in a crazy world.

Realism begins with the dismissal of the *grand illusion*, despair and cynicism. It continues with happiness as the goal of life. But happiness is not possible without realistic hope. There are four very important mental reinforcements for appropriate expectations. They keep us on the track to sanity.

RESISTANCE TO PURITY

Many people are looking for what they can never find. They are looking for "the right decision." This "right decision," in their mind, is one that is morally pure. It embraces the good. It refuses to have anything to do with evil. It is absolutely, unequivocally right.

Moral purists have a hard time staying sane, happy or hopeful. They are perpetually frustrated. No matter what decision they make it always has some bad consequence or other. Good is always mixed with evil. The positive is always entangled with the negative. The traditional world of "right" and "wrong" does not seem to exist in reality.

> Herb is a married man with two homes- his own and the home of his lover. Marge is his lover. She brings an enormous joy and fulfillment to his life. Herb knows that his life would be far happier if only Marge and he could marry and live together. But he has two children who love and adore their father, who are emotionally very vulnerable and who would be harmed by his separation from their mother. No matter what he chooses to do somebody is going to get hurt.

> Louise has been diagnosed with a fatal cancer. She is terrified of the truth and needs to pretend that everything will be alright. Through the years she promised her house to a woman companion who has been a faithful support to her for over a quarter of a century. She has refused to write a

will because she does not want to deal with the painful issue of death. If she dies with no will, distant relatives will inherit the house. Making her confront her impending death will traumatize her. But failing to do it will be to allow a terrible injustice to take place.

Ralph, a longtime and devoted employee of an auto parts company, no longer has the skills needed for his job. He is limited and unable to master the changing technology. The company is not rich enough to be generous. It is struggling to survive. Dismissing him after many years of loyal service will destroy him. But letting him stay endangers the future of the company. No matter what decision the company makes something positive and something negative happens.

These three "dilemmas" are not bizarre exceptions to decision making. They are examples of the ordinary decisions that ordinary people have to make every day. Choosing is rarely choosing the good alternative over the bad alternative. It is weighing advantages over disadvantages and trying to figure out which decision will yield the most favorable positive balance.

There is no magical formula that will eliminate disadvantages. Love does not conquer all. The troubled lover and father cannot follow his romantic yearnings without harming his wife and his children. Truth is not always the best policy. Justice for the woman companion will mean a painful emotional agony for the cancerous friend. Compassion is not always the guiding light of life. The employee with obsolete skills stands in the way of the viability of a small company with other workers and other families.

Often life is reduced to choosing between two rotten alternatives. Fighting Hitler and Tojo in a terrible war with the prospect that millions of innocent people will be killed, seems better than the alternative. Taking an experimental chemotherapy for lung cancer, with all its devastating effects on the body, seems better than dying without trying to live.

We are always weighing advantages against disadvantages, good consequences against bad consequences. Life has no paradise of purity. It is just like politics, negotiating between alternatives where no alternative has completely clean hands. Even personal decisions that have little immediate effect on other people are pragmatically ambiguous. Choosing a career is often a trial of torture for many people. What am I best suited for? What will I love doing? What can I do that will guarantee me a well-paying job? If I choose to be a lawyer, I give up the opportunity of being a happy and successful physician. If I choose to be an accountant, I give up my chance of becoming a recognized musician.

Some people choose to console themselves with the thought that there is one and only one thing that they are destined to be. But that is part of the *grand illusion*. The truth of the matter is that each of us is multi-talented. We cannot be everything we are good at. We have to choose. And when we choose, if we are realistic, we know that there is something else we may have chosen to be which would have made us just as happy. There is not enough time in one lifetime to be everything we could be. To do one thing well means that we have to forego doing another thing well.

Some people never expect to escape disadvantages. They do not insist on purity when purity is unavoidable. They never take self-righteous poses, proclaiming that their own decisions are unblemished. On the contrary, they are empathic. They can understand an opposing point of view. They can see the benefits in the decision they rejected. They can talk to people they disagree with without contempt. They know that the right decision is not the perfect decision. It is the choice which, under the circumstances, yields the greatest number of positive results over negative results.

Purists are unhappy people who drive other people crazy. They are paralyzed by all the obvious disadvantages to any decision. Realists know better. They are never intimidated by disadvantages. They know that every good achieved also has its negative side.

AVOIDING GUARANTEES

When I was in Peru some sixteen years ago, I met a very charming young American missionary. He had come down to Lima to do some shopping before he returned to the back country where he sought to convert the Catholic Indians to some branch of Protestant fundamentalism with a *holy-roller* edge. We were in a tourist bus together and had the opportunity to talk leisurely for about two hours. He was thirty-one, unmarried, from Oklahoma, with a clean-cut, all American look, a little nervous and edgy, but calm enough to listen if he had to. I asked him about his work and what made him choose this risky and very different profession. He told me that his parents were academics and non-religious. He was an only child who grew up in a secular home, attended the University of Oklahoma, majored in psychology, became involved in radical politics in the late 60's and then found himself both disillusioned and unemployed after his graduation. It was at that time that he was invited to a prayer meeting. He initially resisted but ultimately went along because he was curious. It was at that meeting that he was "born again." And now, he said he had dedicated his life to God. What made his faith so meaningful to him was that the promise of God was firm where before he had relied on the promises of men. He believed, with all his heart, that the second coming of Christ would take place within a decade and that the world would be transformed. The Bible had spoken. There was no reason to doubt the ultimate fulfillment of its prophecy.

I did not tell him that I was less sure than he was that salvation would take place right away. And I wonder now whether he kept his faith after the crushing disappointment of *no-show*. But his passionate confession to me revealed the kind of promise that many people need in order to cope with life. They want more than possibilities. They want guarantees.

But there are no guarantees. No matter how strong your faith, how intense your intuition, there is no way of knowing for sure that something will happen. The human condition is uncertainty. We want to know what will happen, sometimes desperately want to know. But, from our perspective the future is speculation, not reality. All we can experience is the present. All we can remember is the past. Science and common sense can help us predict the future. But they cannot guarantee it.

> Peter is a young physician who is unable to make a decision to marry. He is in a successful relationship which has lasted for seven years. His lover is a nurturing woman who understands his many shortcomings and is willing to live with them. He is a short-tempered worrier who explodes frequently and requires a great deal of attention. When his lover, weary of waiting for him to *up* the level of commitment, told him that she was not prepared to continue the relationship unless he married her, he panicked. He said that he loved her, that they were perfect complements to each other, and that he was most happy when he was with her. But he wanted to be absolutely sure that everything would turn out alright if he married her. He still needed time.

Obviously people should not rush into marriage, especially if they have important doubts. But what did Peter want? What further proof was required that the relationship would work? What would his life be like if she left him? How does one become absolutely sure about anything? Marrying his lover would be no impulsive act. They knew and understood each other very well. They were, for all practical purposes, leading a successful married life.

Many people linger in the limbo of indecision because they are waiting for what never comes. They are waiting for the moment of absolute certainty. They are waiting for the decision without risk. No matter how much evidence, no matter how convinced they are of the rightness of an action, they cannot endure the inevitable doubts. "What if?" is such a seductive question. Postponement becomes their life style. They always need more time to consider. They crave the assurance of absolute certainty. Life passes them by. By the time they are ready to make a decision they are dead. And, along the way, they drive everybody crazy with their "should I" or "shouldn't I."

Expecting guarantees is futile anxiety. It is a no-win formula for living. It is an unrealistic expectation. It only leads to exhaustion and lost opportunities. Every decision involves some risk. Rational people are not deliberately reckless. They do not plunge for the sake of plunging. But they do not design games for themselves which they are bound to lose. The "guarantee game" is one of those loser games. Realism recommends caution, but not paralysis.

BEYOND RESCUE FANTASIES

When we are born, we are completely helpless. We cannot do anything for ourselves. We are totally dependent on our mother and father. If they should abandon us, we would die. While some people grow up feeling abandoned, feeling that they did not receive all the love and nurturing they needed and deserved, other people grow up with the memory of being rescued by loving parents who responded to their every cry of discomfort. They wailed and somebody came to rescue them and to comfort them. All that they needed to do was to cry and to look pitiable and somebody was there to pick them up and make sure that everything was alright.

Infancy is a very powerful time in our lives. It helps to fashion how we see and deal with our world. Since our childhood is so long (compared to our evolutionary cousins), we never really cease to be children. The skills for survival that we learn as babies stay with us for a long while. If they worked very well for us, we are reluctant to give them up. We keep using them even when we grow up, even when we are adults.

Like many women in traditional environments, Andrea developed very good dependency skills. She was an adorable baby, an only child, whom her parents doted on and catered to. Very early she learned that crying brought them running. They would kiss her and hug her and brush away her tears. Even when she was scolded for doing something wrong, she would burst into tears. Her crying, her vulnerability, her helplessness would turn off their anger. Little children have that power. That is why crying is one of their most effective skills for survival, followed closely by looking pitiable. Most people want to rescue and forgive cute little babies. But Andrea is now sixty and fat. She still cries alot and is very good at looking miserable. And she still hopes that somebody will show up to pick her up, comfort her and take responsibility for her happiness. But she is divorced and alone. And any man who tried to pick her up would rupture himself. Yet her rescue fantasy continues. She is still waiting for her savior to show up. In the interim she has alienated most of her friends who are not prepared to play *mama* to her pitiable child.

Rescue fantasies are among the most powerful inappropriate expectations around. They are the stuff out of which Messiahs and Messianic religions are made. They thrive on infantilized adults who prefer faithful waiting to realism. It is not easy to give up the postures of childhood. The fatal attraction of childhood security produces false hope.

Realism has very little appeal to the Andrea's of the world. It is too harsh and demanding. It has the bad grace to demand that children become adults, that Messiahs be dismissed, that the rituals of dependency be replaced by risky responsibility. In the real world hopeful people know that progress is slow, that two steps forward mean at least one step backward and that no one is saved except by his own efforts alone.

Zionism, the national liberation movement of the Jewish people, rejected the rescue fantasy. Defying the religious tradition of centuries, it proposed to stop waiting for the Messiah and to create an independent Jewish state in Palestine through human determination. While some pioneers moved from religious illusion to Marxist illusion, the overwhelming majority stuck to a slow painful process of settling the land piece by piece. They had no reason to believe in the kindness of the fates. Good fortune was not around for most of Jewish history. Skepticism mixed with enthusiasm produced self-reliance. In the end, they got less land than they wanted and more problems than they could handle. But it was better than "waiting for Godot."

The "end of days" is only another ordinary day with problems. The most we can expect is slow improvement. But when you substitute slow improvement for salvation, human experience can justify optimism.

Political America is now confronting the rescue fantasy. Millions of poor people assaulted by unemployment, underemployment, drugs and crime, see themselves as pitiable figures worthy of rescue. They see themselves as victims of a process over which they have no control. They imagine that the white establishment and the government could save them if they only chose to. Their salvation lies with others. And the responsibility for their salvation lies with others. Rage and despair are the only childlike tools for survival that are left to them.

The failure of our welfare system for the poor is testimony to the rescue fantasy. After sixty years, inherited dependency and collapsing families have devastated the people who need help. Playing the victim, however, realistic, does no good. Until the poor give up the notion of salvation by government, they will not be saved. Only when they assume responsibility for their own lives, struggle for self-reliance, and seek to discipline their own lives and their own neighborhoods will any assistance from government do any good. Realism starts with self-help. We have learned very painfully that neither the government nor the revolution, by themselves, can rescue anybody. They can only help those who choose to help themselves.

BEYOND THE CULT OF INTENTIONS

When I was a chaplain in Korea three years after the truce was arranged, I was overwhelmed by the endless landscape of physical destruction and human misery. I wanted to do something to alleviate suffering. I was not quite sure what to do. But providing food and clothing for war orphans seemed a modest and practical project. I contacted my commanding officer for support. He was enthusiastic about the proposal and assigned an officer to assist me. The officer was a combat engineer, a Tennessee man with a warm smile and an even warmer handshake. He was eager to let me know how much he valued this opportunity to help "little kids" and volunteered to assume responsibility for the Christmas at the orphanage. I was surprised by his almost excessive kindness. Yet I had no reason to doubt his sincerity and gladly turned over the event to his responsibility. I was wrong to have done that. When Christmas came nothing had been done. He had failed to follow through on all his promises. He defended himself by pleading illness. The orphans went hungry. And I was embarrassed and angry.

I was especially angry at myself for my naivety. I had assumed that spoken enthusiasm was the same as real enthusiasm. I did not even question his sincerity at the moment he offered his help. But conscious sincerity and good intentions are not the stuff out of which effective action is fashioned. I had placed too much faith in his words without investigating his behavior. I later discovered that this pattern of negligence was characteristic of everything he did. He got away with it because he was charming and gracious and seemingly well-intentioned. And I had become the unwilling victim of the cult of intentions.

In our present introspective age what people think and feel and want to do is often more important than what they do. Sincerity and good intentions become the core of morality. They also become the perfect excuse for incompetence and negligence. "He meant well" compensates for broken promises and makes disappointment a natural consequence of virtue. Bad intentioned people who help others are "obviously" inferior to good-intentioned people who harm them.

After my Christmas party experience, I became more skeptical and more realistic. I recognized that talk was cheap and that, in the end, only action counted. I paid less attention to what people wanted to do or said they wanted to do and became much more interested in what they did do. I became even less interested in my own conscious intentions and much more attention to what I was prepared to do. It was sobering to discover how much pretense there was in my own life. You can become mesmerized by your own sincerity.

In time my expectations of others changed. I saw little connection between good intentions and good behavior. I discovered that sometimes openly selfish people did more good for others than verbal "bleeding hearts." I became less concerned with motivation and more concerned with results.

Several years ago I met an extraordinary egomaniac at a dinner party. He was a self-made billionaire who could not stop talking about himself and his achievements. He had started out with junk and ended up with a real estate empire. Along the way he had provided jobs for ten thousand people, endowed two science institutes, financed a major inner-city hospital and donated his modern art collection to a major museum. In conversation, he was insufferable. He was obsessed with himself. It was clear that his conscious motivation was fame and recognition. But the results were far more altruistic than the generosity of most of my well-intentioned rich friends who had difficulty parting with pennies. Did I care about his intentions? No. Did I admire his behavior? Yes.

A fellow board member of a charitable organization to which I belong complained to me that our chairman, who had managed to raise over one million dollars for scholarships, was only motivated by personal power. I replied by pointing out that the previous chairman, who was a sincere *nebbish*, had managed to lose four hundred thousand dollars in scholarship grants through his leisurely negligence. There was no doubt that if I had my *druthers* I would prefer efficient intentional saints to efficient intentional egomaniacs. But, if I had to choose between intentions and results, I preferred results.

Ambitious politicians do not turn me off so long as they help their constituents. Self-absorbed parents do not bother me as long as they nurture children. Cynical teachers do not arouse my disdain as long as they elevate the skills of their students. Motivation is so complex that it is difficult to know which intention is the "real" one. To be "pure of heart" and a behavioral disaster is meaningless to me. When the cult of incompetence is wedded to the cult of good intentions only disaster ensues.

The greatest source of illusion is the inability to distinguish between intentions and behavior. So often we think that what we are is what we say we want to be—or that other people are what they say they want to be. Realism is replaced by a naive sincerity.

Sincerity often victimizes us. People ask us what we feel and believe—and we tell them what we sincerely feel and believe—even though what we sincerely think we feel and believe has nothing to do with our own behavior. We—and others—settle for sincerity when what we should be demanding is truth.

Appropriate expectations do not rely on some necessary correlation between saintly motivation and saintly behavior. They prefer to notice competence and strength of will. Maybe, what people really want is what they end up doing.

$\boxed{10}$

TAMING FEAR
Step 5

IN A CRAZY WORLD THERE IS A crazy side to human nature. This crazy side is what we call our emotions. Taking control of our lives means taking control of our emotions.

Emotions are not easy to control. They are very old and independent. They have a life all their own. Long before reason ever saw the light of day they were plugging away at survival. Centered in the oldest part of the brain they have a long head start on rational thinking and realism.

Each of the emotions evolved and survived because it served a useful purpose. Fear helped us avoid danger. Anger kept outsiders from entering our space. Love nurtured the young. Jealousy fostered competition among the fit. Hate expelled undesirables from vulnerable communities. Guilt made us all cooperative.

Feelings are not simple. They are a complex mixture of internal drive, external awareness, muscular tension and overt behavior. They are not merely something inside. They show up in the muscles of our face, the posture of our body and the message of our eyes. Strong feeling is not easily hidden. It starts in the old brain and makes its way to the tips of our fingers and toes.

Feelings are strategies for survival, both for ourselves, for our offspring and for our community. Their problem is that they are not fine-tuned to reality. As human responses to an ever-changing world, they are often too inflexible, too intense, too determined to carry on regardless of consequences. While they provide the passion of life, they also provide one of the major problems of life. They need to be restrained and directed.

Restraining and directing feelings is not easy. They command enormous amounts of energy. They develop their own agenda independent of our general welfare. They are not always compatible, sending out mixed signals and conflicting commands, producing internal tensions and ambivalence. Living with our feelings is often like being driven in different directions at the same time.

The only power we have to control, fashion, and focus our feelings is the power of our reason. Reason is newer than emotion. It has its headquarters in the most recently evolved parts of our brain. It is less intense than feeling, more flexible, more fine-tuned to reality, more aware of the consequences of our actions. Reason is not emotion. But it is intimately connected to emotion. Without the energy of emotion, reason would be passive and dead. It is the fire of feeling that reason both uses and subdues. If we desire nothing, reason has no reason to explore. And if all our desires were compatible, reason would lose its main job of controller and arbiter.

Staying sane in a crazy world means controlling the inner craziness of competing emotions. Our fear struggles with anger. Our love struggles with hate. Our lust struggles with guilt. Only reason can harness their energies and make them work together for common goals. More ventilation accomplishes nothing. From time to time it is comfortable to let off steam, to express pent-up emotions. But we must never forget that the reason many emotions are pent up is because they need to be. If I always give vent to my anger, my jealousy, my hate and my love, unashamedly and spontaneously, then I will end up just as crazy as the world that I live in.

The first and oldest emotion is fear. Fear is a very useful feeling and response. Life is filled with danger. There are so many people and things that can hurt and destroy us. There are so many situations and events that can harm and disable us. Fear helps us run away from the danger, to escape from the threat to our own welfare. Without fear we would be swallowed up by our own enemies.

There are so many real "enemies," pain, helplessness, poverty, crime, humiliation, hostility, illness and death. We need to be careful. Fear is the internal signal of caution. Avoidance, escape and flight flow necessarily from its trigger. The greater the danger, the greater the fear, the faster we run away.

Some dangers are not easy to run away from. They are not concrete and physical. They arise from our vulnerability as children, from the very nature of the human condition. Some fear dependency. Others fear responsibility. Some fear attachment. Others fear abandonment. Some fear possessiveness. Others fear individuality. Our own personal experience determines what we see as dangerous.

Fear is useful. But it can also be harmful. If we see danger where there is no real danger, if we exaggerate the danger and make it more dangerous than it really is, if we come to believe that we are powerless to handle any danger that intrudes on our life, then fear takes over our life and paralyzes us. We become obsessed with danger. We become masters of avoidance. We become victims of fear.

Fear is also embarrassing. For many people to be afraid is a sign of weakness. They would rather confess to almost anything than to fright. Masculine virtue means not only the conquest of fear but also the elimination of fear. Brave men do not fear. When they are asked, "Are you afraid?" they always protest. "Not me, I'm not afraid."

People who are embarrassed by their fear will resort to strange ways of hiding it. They will often plunge into reckless and foolish action in order to prove that they are brave. Or, if they are unable to be brave, they will pretend that they never really wanted what they are too afraid to achieve. We call this rationalization "sour grapes."

Being realistic about fear is essential to sanity. If we are too indulgent and turn everything and everybody into an insurmountable danger, we will live in an illusory world of terror. If we are too embarrassed and hide from our fear, we will spend too much time covering up our feelings and too little time solving our problems. And if we are too eager to be guided by our feelings and not control them, we will pursue their agenda and not our own. Taming fear is part of training for realism.

RECOGNIZING DANGER

Hannah fell in love with a young student from Saudi Arabia. She was thirty-five years old, an English teacher in high school and eager to get married before she was too old to get a husband. He was thirty-years old, a student in electrical engineering at a local university and a devout Muslim. He told her that he planned to return to Saudi Arabia after graduation and to live their permanently. He was sure that she would be able to adjust to the Muslim life style. He said that his mother was a progressive woman who knew how to get around burdensome restrictions on women and to live quite happily. Friends pointed out to her that moving to Saudi Arabia for an American woman was a dangerous venture, especially if she was intending to be "domesticated," entering into the domestic life of the Muslim population. The treatment of women was radically different from what she was accustomed to. If she was unhappy, she might find it very difficult to escape. Hannah said she was not concerned. She felt confident that she could handle any problem that would arise. She was sure that, if she wanted to leave, nobody would be able to stop her, since her will was very strong. Although her friends admired her courage, they felt that she was recklessly naive, setting herself up for trauma. They were right. One year after the marriage, Hannah telephoned one of her friends hysterical. She was pregnant and terrified. She was forbidden contact with any member of her family until the baby was born. Because she wanted to leave, she feared for her life. Her dream marriage had turned into a nightmare. She had failed to be realistic about the dangers that confronted her.

Too much caution takes the joy out of life. But too little caution can lead to disaster. It is not true that courage and determination conquer all. It is not true that all problems are surmountable, all dangers are resistible, all provocations are confrontable. There are certain situations we should never voluntarily enter into, especially if people do not share our vision of personal rights.

The trapped woman was a victim of her bravado and over-confidence. She did not want to admit her limitations. She was no different from my overweight and overage friend who suffered a heart attack playing too fiercely on the squash court, or my neighbor, a prominent obstetrician, striving to be eternally young, who fell off his teenage son's motorcycle and broke his ankle.

The human condition imposes limitations. It is foolish to ignore them.

> Felice did. She was a painter with an incredible eye for the wonders of nature. She loved cigarettes and smoked incessantly. When friends expressed their concern, she would reassure them by saying that her grandfather, a chain smoker, had lived to ninety. "It's all in the genes" she would say. On her fiftieth birthday she discovered that she had lung cancer. Eighteen months later she died after intense suffering. One week before she died she confessed, "I thought I was special. I thought it wouldn't happen to me."

We all imagine that we are invulnerable. Our limitations oppress us and we like to tease the fates. But the fates are blind and dumb laws of nature which grind out their "punishment" with no glimmer of awareness of whom they sweep away. You cannot tease the fates. They do not care. Only we care.

> Every action has its consequences. Fred, who is an AIDS activist knows that. He stood before the television camera gaunt and somewhat weary. Very open and very honest, he described the life style of promiscuous sex he had indulged for over five years. He had thrown caution to the winds,

found excitement in the pleasures of the moment and loved every moment of his dance with danger. In the back of his mind, he had come to believe that his actions would have no consequences. He despised the overreactions of fearful gays. He admired adventure. In the end he became a victim of his own bravado.

There are moments in life when the courage to risk death on behalf of some noble cause seems worthwhile. But not when all that follows is senseless suffering.

NO EXAGGERATION

One of the ways to make ourselves important is to give ourselves important enemies. If our foes are significant we are significant by association. That is the appeal of paranoia. We must be important if powerful people hate us so much.

Exaggerating danger is very appealing. Not only does it sometimes boost our ego. It also gives us the excuse to do nothing. If dangers are overwhelming, then taking risks is foolish. If enemies are formidable, then offering resistance is foolish. Where there is no chance of success, there is no reason to act.

One of my students was preparing to give his first speech on a public stage. The thought of standing up before an audience of his peers and his family filled him with terror. He spent sleepless nights imagining hostile people booing him and chasing him off the stage. His anxiety was so intense that he called me up to tell me that he was too sick to speak on the day of his performance. I told him that he was not sick and that he would be branded a coward by his peers if he did not show up. When he arrived at the hall, I assured him that the audience was not out to get him. At worst they would yawn. At best they would applaud. His anxiety seemed to lessen. When he came out on the stage he was ready for rejection. But when he opened his mouth the audience listened. After fifteen minutes a few senior citizens got up and quietly left. But almost all the audience stayed to hear what the student had to say. At the end of the speech there was quiet applause. He had imagined the worst and the worst had not happened. He had survived the ordeal in tact. The danger had been exaggerated.

There are many dangers that look bigger than they really are. If we see ourselves as very small and very vulnerable then our foe looms large by contrast. If we always see ourselves as children then adult authorities look too big for challenge. We fear that their disapproval will kill us.

Gary is a successful accountant. He is thirty-five, very athletic, big and strong, with a booming voice. His mother is only five feet tall, somewhat arthritic and speaks with a ludicrous whine. But Gary is afraid of her. He is afraid to tell her that he is in love, that he wants to get married and that he wants to move out of the house. In his eyes she is nine feet tall, with the strength of an Amazon and the power to erase him from the face of the earth with one little disapproval. Gary's vision of his mother comes from infancy. It has never changed, even though he has grown taller and his mother has shrunk. In his eyes the consequence of her rejection is death. No one has the power over him she has. If he could see his mother as she really is, the reward would be his liberation.

When I was in the sixth grade I had a teacher whose reputation was terrifying. No one tangled with Miss Pierce and survived.

When she walked into the classroom her glare was enough to shut every mouth and to produce a stonier than stony silence. I always remembered her as big and tall with penetrating dark eyes. Twenty years after my graduation from elementary school I encountered her in a department store. I was surprised when I saw her. She was short and thin with gentle blue eyes. I knew that she was Miss Pierce. She looked so weak and vulnerable. Why was I so afraid?

Our childhood makes us exaggerate. When we grow up our minds sometimes do not follow our bodies. Everything in our vision is out of proportion. Parents and teachers and community leaders intimidate us and make us conform even when we do not want to conform. The body is the body of an adult. But the eyes are the eyes of a child. Even bosses and judges look like our parents and fill us with dread. We cannot take charge of our life because other more powerful people are in charge of it. Only when we break the magic spell, when we are able to see the people of our childhood as neither gods nor devils can we be strong enough to be free.

ACCEPTING FEAR

Getting rid of all fear is an illusion. Brave people do not get rid of their fear. They control it. Heroes are not fearless. There is nothing courageous about courting danger if you do not fear it.

Mary Queen of Scots was reported to have said just before her beheading, "I do not fear death, because I know that I will soon be with God in heaven." Is this smug response to annihilation more courageous than my agnostic soldier friend who won a Bronze Star for valor at the Battle of the Bulge and who told me that just before the battle "I thought that this was going to be the end."

Fear is fear. It is eminently human. It is a perfectly respectable emotion. If it is appropriate to the danger it has no reason to be ashamed. It will not go away so long as the danger is there. Being afraid is no sign of weakness. It is no justification for self-reproach. It is the sign of our being alive and responsive to the world around us. Fearless people are not real people.

Pretending to be unafraid when we are afraid is harmful. We cannot deal with our fears effectively nor control them unless we admit their existence. Emotions are emotions. They cannot be dismissed. They cannot be commanded to leave. They are simply there. All we can do is to act on them or resist them. If our fears are exaggerated, we need to shrink them. But we do not need to eliminate them. They are useful tools for survival.

Audiences should not terrify us. But they should scare us enough so that we train our talents. Parents should not dominate us. But their disapproval should intimidate us enough so that we take the time to listen to them. Teachers should not silence us. But there should be enough fear so that we can learn their wisdom.

Several years ago I encountered a poet who, like most poets, had trouble finding a publisher and even an audience to listen to his poetry. He told me that he did not fear rejection. He had no need for the approval of others. All that he valued was the creative act itself. If people valued his poetry, "fine." And if they did not value it, "fine." It was a matter of indifference to him whether others liked what he created. He paid no attention to the opinions of peers. He ignored the critiques of local writers. An artist lived only for his art, not for the fickle approval of fickle people.

I told him that I did not believe him. His indifference was unreal and a pose. I told him that he was so afraid of adverse criticism that he pretended not to care, and that he was so needy for an audience that he hid from his need with this romantic version of the artist standing alone. If he was so indifferent to the opinions of others, why did he want me to read his poetry and why did he defend it when I offered negative criticism?

An honest artist knows that he wants to be valued. He fears rejection by those he respects. He does not pretend that other people's opinions are unimportant. He does not have to waste his energy in hiding from his fear and from his needs. It is perfectly normal to want approval and enthusiasm for the things we create. It is perfectly normal to fear hostility and derision. The strength to live with hostility and derision can only come from knowing that we fear it. We cannot control the fear if we do not admit that it exists. Pretending to be indifferent is a useless pose that requires enormous effort. It is much easier to acknowledge our fear and to put it in its place.

We do not need to get rid of fear. We need to acknowledge it and use it. When it points to real danger, we need to pay attention to it. When it points to illusory danger, we need to understand it. When it exaggerates, we need to tame it. When it interferes with long-run goals, we need to resist it. But we never hide from it. It is much too exhausting to do that. It only makes us look silly and pretentious.

A tourist guide once told me that he was afraid to fly even though he had to fly all the time with the groups he accompanied. He said that he initially pretended that he was not afraid because he was ashamed of his fear. But the harder he tried to hide from his fear the more it obsessed him. One day, in desperation, he admitted to himself that he was afraid. It was as though a heavy burden had fallen from his shoulders. "Now that I know my fear is there, I can resist it," he said. Taming fear begins with the admission that there is something there to tame.

DEVELOPING PRIORITIES

Stress comes from fear. The body is on the alert for danger all the time. If we see more and more danger we become more and more afraid. Sometimes there is so much fear that it becomes intolerable. Overload is a common experience, especially in an overcrowded, fast-paced, urban world where time and space are of the essence.

Moderate stress gives meaning to life. Problems make us afraid and we need to confront them. Challenges appear and we accept them. We make demands on ourselves and frighten ourselves with schedules and deadlines. Both work and leisure sponsor the fear of failure. But if the challenges were not there, if existence were only peace and quiet, if dramatic change vanished, the landscape of our life would be boring. Floating in the womb may be some people's vision of paradise. But, it is only really great for a vacation.

Excessive stress, on the other hand, is self-destructive. Something good turns into something bad. There is too much danger. There is too much fear. There are too many provocations. We do not know which problem to deal with first. We feel overwhelmed.

Realistic people do not seek to eliminate stress, just as they do not seek to eliminate fear. They seek to diminish it. They want to find that proper balance between boredom and burnout. When stress becomes excessive, when there are too many dangers to deal with, they know that they cannot handle all the problems simultaneously. The anticipation of doing that is the trigger to collapse. They know that they need a schedule of fear. If they can handle their problems one by one, they can manage them. If they have to confront them all together, they will not survive.

A schedule of fear means a consciously chosen priority list. I will deal with this problem first and not that problem. I will confront this danger now and that one later. Priority lists are artificial, but they are indispensable to sanity. A crazy world gives us more problems than we can handle. But we do not have to be equally crazy and arrange for failure.

> Laura is a divorcee. She was abandoned by her physician husband after she worked to put him through two residencies and a post-doctoral fellowship. She is the mother of two young children, one of whom suffers from a rare kidney disease requiring constant attention. The middle school at which she teaches mathematics is being closed, with no guarantee to the teachers of future employment. As an only child, she is the sole guardian of her ailing, widowed mother, who is very dependent on Laura as she was on Laura's father. Laura's own health is fragile. She suffers chronic back pain which has been aggravated by the stress of her personal situation. She gets up in the morning and panics. She does not know what to do first. Laura cannot handle all her problems simultaneously. She cannot tend to her children, work, look for employment, cater to her mother, watch her health and search for a new partner all at once. She has to figure out what comes first and what comes last. She also has to determine how to tune out the hostility and disappointment of dependent people who demand more than she is prepared to give. The act of making a priority list reduces her anxiety and makes what seems unmanageable manageable. She chooses her children first, her search for employment second, her mother third, her conscientiousness at her present job fourth. Her back pain and her loneliness she leaves for future programming. She divides her energies according to her plan. Her current principal is not

happy. Nor is her mother. But Laura is back in charge of her life.

Making choices, putting your life in order, means that you cannot have everything that you want, that you cannot solve every problem you confront, that you cannot please everybody that you need approval from. Fighting overload means enduring some failure in order to achieve some success.

Ken is a chemist. He is a leading researcher for a major auto company. He lives and breathes his work, sometimes investing seven days a week in the testing of future developments. He loves his job and loves being on the cutting edge of the new technology. But his marriage of ten years is rocky. He rarely sees his wife and six year old son. He wants to be close to them, to be involved in their lives. But the demands of his work always draw him away. His wife does not work outside the house. She is very domestic, finding her work identity in managing the house and being a mother. Family is the most important value in her life and she feels cheated. She threatens divorce. Ken panics. He contemplates a less exciting, less demanding, more routine research job, which would free him to spend evenings and weekends with his wife and son. But the thought of giving up his present work depresses him. He sticks with his dilemma, desperately trying to juggle work and family. The tension almost leads to his emotional breakdown. What saves his sanity is the realistic awareness that he cannot have his cake and eat it too. He has to make a choice. He can succeed at the work he loves or the family he loves, but he cannot succeed at both. He chooses his work. That is his first love. He is now separated from his wife and planning divorce. The thought of failing at fatherhood pains him. But he feels in control of his life and continues to love his job. He is dating a career woman. She does not want children. He does not have everything he wants. Yet a partial success is better than paralysis.

Priority lists do not give us all that we need or desire. They do not cope satisfactorily with every danger we confront. But they force us to develop a perspective on life. They help us keep what we fear most to lose.

CHOOSING COURAGE

In the nineteenth century writers and intellectuals spent a great deal of time discussing the importance of will. From Nietzsche to Shaw, the people whose will was strong were the role models for humanity. What they meant by will was a certain boldness and decisiveness that flowed from the energy of life. Parents and teachers also lectured on will. They meant something less dramatic by it. They meant a conscious determination to act in the face of both risk and responsibility. Both notions of will are close to each other. In Freudian terms the will is the instrument of the ego, the expression of the reality principle, which disciplines our desire in the name of survival. Will is control.

Today there is very little discussion of will. People are more introspective. Psychotherapy has taken its toll. Strengthening your will is no longer fashionable. In fact, it sounds somewhat old-fashioned. Getting in touch with your feelings is important. Understanding why you do what you do is important. Responding to your inner voice is important. The problem with all this introspection is that it post-pones action. It makes people turn inward. It makes people say, "When I am in the mood I will do it."

But what if the right mood never comes? What if waiting for the right mood means eternal waiting? What if thinking about your feelings day after day is depressing? What if the inner journey is an endless trip to nowhere, leading you farther and farther away from the problems you have to solve?

Many people believe that behavior follows feeling. Inner courage comes before outer courage. We have to feel brave first before we can act bravely. Getting your inner house in order is nec-essary before you can do anything about the outer world. A long and grueling introspection is needed before you experience the conquest of fear.

> Mary is a young woman. She has trouble making deci-sions. She cannot figure out what college to enroll in. The thought of picking a major terrifies her. She is hesitant to commit herself to any course of study. She can handle living together with her boyfriend but not marriage. She attends countless weekend marathons. She is always think-ing about her feelings and discussing them. She finds med-itation profound. Her decision? Life is always *mañana.* Whenever she is confronted with an important decision, she says, "It doesn't feel right." Her life is on hold.

Mary is a victim of will deprivation. She is lost in a sea of feel-ings, many of them fears. She imagines that by studying them, think-ing about them and living with them intimately, they will have a mes-sage for her. But endless introspection without action is a guaranteed road to depression. Sedentary self-analysis is often a prelude to endless waiting. People wait and wait for the right feeling, or the right mood, or the right inner voice. When the right feeling arrives then they will take action. But it often never shows up. And so the waiting continues. Waiting is depressing. No action comes from endless waiting.

Will deprivation can only be countered by a different way of looking at feelings. It may not be the case that behavior follows feeling. It may be the case that feeling follows behavior. First we do something when we are not in the mood, we do it well, and our mood changes. We do not wait for our fear to go away and then act courageously. We act while we are still afraid, and then our fear diminishes because we are successful.

Courage is not an introspective victory. It is an act of will. We choose to act in the middle of our fear, with all the risks that decision entails. If we win, we will become less afraid. If we lose, we may become more afraid. But no one can tame fear with guarantees.

If you wait to lose your fear of the water before you plunge, you will never swim. If you wait to lose your fear of heights before you descend, you will never ski. If you wait to lose your fear of audiences before you speak, you will never speak.

Peter was a young man who came to interview me ten years ago about my philosophy. He was a student at a local university who was curious about what a rational approach to living would mean and wanted to write a paper about it. He spoke English with a Slavic accent, and I asked him where he was born. He said Russia. I asked him how he had come to this country. He said that he had defected from a Russian dance troupe that had come to New York. I expressed my admiration for his courage. He told me that he was not very brave. He simply did what he had to do. But he told me that what helped him to defect was a lesson he had learned when he first began dancing in Russia. Before his first public performance he was so nervous that he started to cry. His teacher tried to comfort him and said to him, "Peter, if you do not perform, you will be more nervous because you will never know how good you are. But if you do perform, you will discover that you can dance and that people like your dancing and you will be less afraid." "That's exactly what happened," he said. "And so I knew when the opportunity to defect came my way, and I was very afraid of being apprehended, that I could not wait to be less afraid. I would have to act right away. Many of my friends wanted to do what I chose to do. But they were waiting to be brave. I chose to act while I was still a coward. And now I am free."

11

USEFUL ANGER
Step 6

"I'M SO ANGRY," THE YOUNG MAN in the hospital said. He was sitting up in bed with his arms folded against his chest, a kind of defiant and defensive posture at the same time. He looked healthy, but he was very sick. His doctors had just informed him that he had a stomach cancer and would require immediate surgery. "It's not fair. I've done everything right. I exercise. I don't smoke. I watch my weight. I'm a vegetarian. I meditate. This shouldn't be happening to me. But it is. And I'm mad. And I'm not quite sure whom I should be mad at. How do you tell God off? I don't know what to do with my feelings."

Anger is a powerful emotion. It is a very old emotion, going far back in evolutionary time. It is not an easy feeling to control. If the provocation is sufficiently strong, it can easily turn into rage.

Anger is the other side of fear. Both anger and fear deal with danger. Fear helps us to run away from danger. Anger helps us to stand our ground, to confront the danger. Defiance is the outer expression of anger. It says to the enemy, "Stop where you are. Do not come any closer. You are treading on my survival."

Anger is older than love. It began with one-celled organisms which expelled intruders from their space. It evolved into complex animals who defined their territory and kept invaders out. They barked, they howled, they bared their teeth. They made aggressive lunges. No one would pass without a fight. After all, space and territory meant food and security. And food and security meant life.

Anger is very human. Without it we would never defend our own personal space. We would allow other people to step all over us. We would have no dignity. Anger defends our dignity. It defines the limits that other people must observe. If we have little anger we turn into a *nebbish* or a luckless martyr.

So many things provoke our anger—physical assaults, verbal insults, aggressive intrusion, cruelty, humiliation and undeserved wrongs. And when we get angry our whole body tenses up. The adrenalin flows. Our heart beats faster. Our gaze becomes focused and intense. We are *revved up* for action and resistance. The enemy will not pass.

Anger, like all the other emotions, is not finely tuned to reality. It tends to develop its own agenda, regardless of the consequences to survival and happiness. Its defiance grows more intense, fueled by the tremendous energy the body devotes to it. Once unleashed it is not always easy to control. Evolution does not always do a perfect job. Rationality is too young and too weak.

Of course, there are old ways of turning off anger. If the enemy surrenders and looks pitiable, anger tends to die down. Fearful children and obsequious servants usually know how to appease parents and masters. It is hard to hit somebody who looks helpless and who does not return our defiance. But if the enemy is equally aggressive, anger can turn into an uncontrollable rage. We lose our *cool*. In war, this rage may lead to acts of extraordinary bravery. In ordinary life, it generally leads to assaults that never should have taken place, to words that never should have been uttered.

Anger can turn into craziness. It can make a crazy world even crazier. It can lead to losing control of your life. It can lead to self-destructive consequences which cannot easily be reversed. But if we express no anger we will be doormats, victims of the exploitation of other people who will abuse us and deprive us of our dignity.

Staying sane means discovering that reasonable balance between martyrdom and uncontrollable rage. If we are too appeasing we will be self-sacrificing "servants." If we are too aggressive, we will alienate the people we need for support and survival. Our reason becomes the arbiter, weighing one set of consequences against another—and doing it fairly quickly since anger does not give us a lot of time to make decisions.

Some people find a virtue in martyrdom. They regard anger as the enemy, the root of all evil. Self-sacrifice is the noble way to live. Dying for others, giving up your wealth to others, paying no attention to your happiness and survival are the signs of saints. Many religions cultivate this life style. Suffering is more virtuous than defiance. Passivity is a sign of childlike faith which God admires.

Of course, if martyrdom is the best path to happiness in the next life, then it makes sense. Intense pain now leads to eternal pleasure later. But if there is no afterlife, if self-destruction leads no

further than self-destruction, then full-time appeasement is profoundly irrational. Aggressive evil cannot be checked by our doing
what it wants us to do.

Martyrdom is different from the strategy of passive disobedience. Non-violent defiance is often an act of clear defiance. Both
Gandhi and Martin Luther King, Jr. understood this. Where the
enemy is often well-armed, the best way to defy him is to use the
power of non-cooperation. If nobody goes to work, if nobody pays
his taxes, if everybody blocks the arteries of transportation, society
grinds to a halt. With an enemy that is less than ruthless such action
is a form of clever and controlled anger. It seeks to humiliate the
enemy by proving his incompetence or by provoking him to outrageous unacceptable cruelty. Passive disobedience works with Britons
and Americans. It would never work with Nazis.

The task of being clever about anger is the task of the realistic
and rational person. Realistic people defend their dignity. They
strive to achieve that happy marriage of anger and reason. They
want to live—but not at any price. And they do not want to die—simply because someone calls it saintly. They know that controlling
anger is essential to sanity.

ACCEPTING ANGER

The other day I was late for an appointment. The man I was supposed
to meet waited an hour for me. When I finally arrived at the restaurant where we had planned to have lunch he was seething. Anger spoke
from every muscle of his body. He attempted a smile, but was not very
successful at it. I knew that he was reluctant *to tell me off* because he
needed some important information from me that no one else could

give him. When I said to him, "I'm sorry. I know that you must be angry," he denied it.

His denial came from more than his fear of offending me. He was a proud man and he was uncomfortable being angry. Anger frightened him. He saw it as some kind of moral defeat or embarrassing weakness. Because he would not admit to himself that he was angry, he could not control it. Although he tried to be pleasant, he became overly rude, contradicting me, even telling me that I did not know what I was talking about. I never did tell him what he wanted to know. If he had only acknowledged his anger, he would have been able to rein it in. You cannot tame a force you refuse to see.

So many people are uncomfortable being angry. They like to imagine that they are above such an emotion, that nothing can provoke them, that they are essentially "cool." Or they feel guilty about having their feelings of indignation, imagining that decency and anger are incompatible. Or they are afraid of their anger, afraid of what they might do if they ever admitted to their rage.

When people deny their anger, it does not go away. It continues to pursue its agenda without any conscious control and without any thought for the consequences of its action. It becomes a blind force in the hands of a blind man. No one can see what needs to be seen.

Anger is a normal human emotion. It is nothing to be ashamed of. It is often useful, an instrument of defense against the aggressiveness of others. As a response to perceived danger it is no more dangerous than fear, and often more appropriate than love. Loving our enemies is an unnatural act. Confronting our enemies, especially if we believe our cause to be just, makes more sense. When we are too passive and accepting in the face of humiliation, we do not need to applaud our surrender. We need to be ashamed that we are not angrier.

Recognizing our anger is not hard to do. Emotions are not ethereal feelings. They are built into the fabric of our body. We can feel our anger in our tense muscles, our clenched teeth, our confrontational posture. All we have to do is to pay attention to our bodies. Others often do. Since they are not caught up in denial, they can see our emotions better than we can.

I still remember the nun who worked with me on a project to raise money to re-open two inner city libraries. Her whole life had been the Church. She had decided to become a nun at the age of eleven. She joined a teaching order, subordinated her will to the discipline of her sisterhood, and had been faithfully obedient for forty years. But she had a falling out with her immediate superior over her political activity. Her punishment was dismissal as a principal of an inner city elementary parochial school and her transfer to a parish school in northern Michigan. When I came to console her, she burst out crying. Her tears were tears of anger. She confessed to me that she felt betrayed after all those years of loyal service. Her removal was outrageous. But the hardest thing for her to do, she said, was to admit that she was angry. Being angry at the Church made her feel guilty. But she felt strangely liberated. She had never been able to admit her anger before. It conflicted with the pious image she had created for herself. Now, for the first time she could stare her anger in the face and name it for what it was.

I could sense both her discomfort and her relief. She was relieved of the burden of hiding her resentment, of using her energy to cover up her rage. Pretending not to mind the minor and major humiliations which her superiors had inflicted on her had been exhausting. She was now free to be angry, even though she was unable or unwilling to do anything about it. She was enraged and she had every right to be. A short while later after she left the order and became a lay teacher. She had found her anger and was able to act on her discovery.

USING ANGER

Our anger is a positive emotional resource. We need to use it wisely. As long as we control its energy, it can give us something no other emotional strategy can provide. It can protect and defend our dignity.

> Otto is an old acquaintance. He had lived for many years as a recluse, unable to establish an ongoing and effective relationship with a woman. When Gloria entered his life he was already forty, painfully shy and very needy. Gloria was married, but separated from her husband. Her two grown sons had worked hard to reconcile their parents. But to no avail. Although Gloria and Otto began to live together shortly after they met, Gloria continued to spend time with her husband and children. Her husband was willing to wait for her to return. He hoped that the pull of children and grandchildren would bring them back together again. Otto naturally objected, asked Gloria to divorce her husband, and proposed marriage. Gloria refused although she insisted that she loved Otto very much. After ten years of this rather bizarre arrangement, Otto had grown very attached to Gloria. He felt deeply committed to the relationship even though marriage was not possible. He could not imagine being without her. One day Gloria's two children came to

visit her. They pleaded with her to leave Otto and to come back to live with their father. They spoke of how uncomfortable it was for their children not to have a real grandparents' home to visit. They hoped that Gloria would come with them "right now" as a sign that things were going to be different. Gloria succumbed to their assault. She penned a short note to Otto, packed her things and left to return to her husband. Otto was hurt and bewildered. He felt betrayed. He still loved Gloria. He tried to understand her agony and could even empathize with the decision she made. He even hoped that she might change her mind. He was prepared to wait for her to return. He saw no reason to be angry. What good would it do?

But being angry was exactly what he needed to be. If, after ten years of love, loyalty and devotion, all that he was worthy of was a short note and quick departure, then he was a doormat, not a lover. What about *his* feelings? What about *his* needs? What about *his* continued willingness to comply with the setup that she had designed for her convenience? Where was his sense of outrage at being abandoned? After all, love was not only a feeling. It was also a behavior. Of what value was love if it was a prelude to masochism? What he needed to do was to take control of his life. Waiting for Gloria to take the initiative would depress him and take away the last vestige of his dignity. He was worthy of a much better relationship, one that had a chance to work—and of a much better partner, someone who treated him with respect and compassion.

There are times when anger is appropriate. To avoid it is to compromise your dignity and to surrender your self-esteem. Otto had grown up to accept whatever life dished out. It was as though destiny was always right, as though the people who abuse you always have legitimate reasons for their abuse, as though to understand is always to forgive. What he needed to do was to say, "There are limits to what you can do to me. And if you do not observe those limits, you will be the rightful recipient of my anger."

NEVER WASTING ANGER

Two years ago I was a passenger in a limousine with a hired driver who was taking me and three others to the Newark Airport from Princeton. While on the expressway a car speeding by failed to signal and jumped into our lane right in front of the limousine. Our driver braked in time, a few objects fell to the floor and the four of us were awakened out of our daydreams. What followed, however, was bizarre. Our driver, furious at the recklessness of the driver of the other car, began to chase him. He sped faster and faster to overtake him. I protested but my protest fell on deaf ears. Our driver was consumed with anger. He was determined to punish the offending "criminal." When the limousine did overtake the other car, our driver forced the "guilty" automobile to the side of the road, jumped out of the car, and ran to the trapped vehicle. He began to curse and scream at the bewildered "criminal" who turned out to be a blasé teenager out for a little joy ride. When he finished with his screaming, he returned to the limousine, sat down, apologized for the outburst, and resumed our slow steady pace to the airport.

I asked the driver why he had bothered to pursue the teenager, since he was not a policeman, and since he did not have the authority to punish him. He replied in the best "weekend marathon" language of the sixties that he needed "to ventilate." He was so mad that he had "to let it out."

Ventilating feelings, letting "everything out" that bothers

you has now become a legitimate pasttime among many contemporary psychotherapists. Bottling up feelings is bad for you. Feeling free to express your anger is good for you. Restraint is a harmful legacy from an "up tight" past. The premise of this approach is that holding in is more exhausting than letting go.

The alternative approach challenges this assumption. It recognizes that expressing anger drains our energies. Getting angry and acting on it is exhausting—more exhausting than getting angry and not acting on it. It is especially exhausting when the anger is wasted, when no positive consequence ensues, when our anger is directed to strangers who do not care about our anger. Screaming at indifferent people is not therapeutic. It is frustrating. Our driver did not feel better and more satisfied because he had pursued the anonymous teenager and told him off. He was hoarse from hollering and weary from the chase. The teenager was more bewildered than intimidated. The pursuit was silly and irrational. It was an exercise in futility. The main victim was the "ventilating driver."

Wasting anger is an emotionally expensive enterprise. Ranting and raving at every person who intrudes on your space and makes you angry is a form of self-destruction. Realistic people are selective. They act out their anger only when their anger will do some good. They see no virtue in unlimited ventilation.

Realistic people do not provoke anger needlessly. Fifteen years ago I crossed over from West Berlin to East Berlin. The crossing was grueling. The East German border guards enjoyed their power and subjected the crossers to humiliating delays. To get into East Berlin you had to endure the waiting and keep your mouth shut. The man in front of me was impatient. He was furious about the unnecessary waiting. He went up to one of the guards and complained angrily. The next thing I knew, he was seized and taken away. He had needlessly provoked the authorities. He was practicing neither civil disobedience nor creative defiance. He was guilty of stupidity, a kind of self-destructive punishment that is neither courageous nor therapeutic.

Realistic men and women do not direct their anger to people who will not pay any attention to it. Realistic people do not become enraged at inanimate objects. They do not kick doors and break glass. They do not lecture earthquakes and denounce behaviors. Above all they do not get angry at the universe. The universe is mainly a collection of inanimate objects and inanimate events. This collection can neither see angry people nor hear angry complaints. In a meaningless universe, telling God off is like talking to the wall. No one is listening. And if someone is listening, he does not care. Realists are spared the agony of arguing with destiny. They accept what they cannot change and change what they are able to. They use their anger sparingly and only when it will do some good.

MAINTAINING YOUR COOL

One of the basic principles of sanity is never to lose your *cool*. Losing your *cool* is losing. When you are in a rage you will generally say and do things that you will later regret. Reason goes out the window. The agenda of relentless anger prevails.

Some "ventilationists" think that periodic explosions drain the emotional system of poisonous, stored-up anger. A good venting of anger now and then relieves depression. People who cannot express their anger turn their anger inward and immobilize themselves. Some therapists arrange for patients to scream, to hit pillows, to denounce "enemies." Catharsis follows. Temporary relief provides some comfort.

But, in real life, rage is a boring strategy. Rage means losing control. It means giving up the agenda of happiness and survival and surrendering to the tyranny of a third emotion. Feeling out of control is more dangerous than feeling *up tight*. There are moments in life when it is appropriate to be loose and relaxed. But there are also other times when it is appropriate to be on the alert and *up tight*.

Cool is a balance between loose and *up tight*. It is coping with craziness without going crazy. *Cool* people are neither cold nor unemotional. They simply have their emotions under control. While they are open to spontaneity and impulse, they are not prepared to sacrifice their long-run interests on the altar of short-term catharsis. They despise emotional exhibitionism, where people feel free to emote without any thought of the consequences—and where honesty and sincerity are excuses for any assault.

> Betty is no example of *cool*. She prides herself on living by impulse. She believes that getting in touch with your feelings, acknowledging them and acting on them is the key to a happy life. She claims that she values openness and honesty above anything else. She has already been through three marriages and has alienated most of her friends. Openness for Betty means uninhibited communication. You simply share everything you are thinking and feeling. "If your friend is truly your friend, he will not mind the truth. He will welcome whatever you have to say, no matter how painful." Betty is famous for her rages. When she gets very mad, she calls up her friends and tells them exactly what she thinks of them. Once she called her best friend, a well-known painter, denounced her for failing to pay enough attention to her, and then proceeded to call her a "hack artist." When the painter, deeply hurt, broke off the relationship,

Betty's response was to defend herself and to complain that most people were not strong enough to handle her honesty. Of course, she failed to mention that if her remaining friends had chosen to be completely honest with her, she too would not have been able to handle it.

No matter how strong we think we are, we all have fragile egos. If all the people whose approval we need, told us exactly what they thought of us—no holds barred—we would be devastated. We all have weaknesses and failings, physical defects and embarrassing behaviors. We know that our friends see them. But we do not expect our friends to talk about them to our face. We ignore each other's "pimples" as an act of kindness. Otherwise honesty becomes an act of cruelty. So many savage verbal assaults are justified in the name of sincerity. Jealous and angry people often claim to be honest when they are only being mean.

When we are *cool* we choose to be both kind and discreet. We share with others what is tolerable. If we wish to preserve friendships we do not tell our friends that they are ugly, have bad taste and are stupid. We reserve that communication for the people we hate. Words are not only informational, they are also judgmental. They have the power to destroy as well as heal. And once uttered they cannot be called back and forgotten.

Uncontrolled anger is the enemy of *cool*. Its power breaks down all the small defense networks that protect relationships and make them work. In the heat of anger we want to be cruel. Negative judgments, which our *cool* has kept safely locked away, come pouring out. They are weapons of assault. They are intended to hurt. They adorn themselves with self-righteous claims to "honest feeling" and "honest grievances." But they are often distortions of feeling which the passion of the moment uses for its purpose.

When I was living in the dormitory at the University of Michigan, I had a roommate who was enormously funny and good company. But he was an incorrigible slob. Clothing, coke bottles, books and papers were strewn everywhere. The good part of him outweighed the bad part of him—and I was determined to maintain the relationship. But it took self-control. I had to accept what I could not change.

One evening I returned from classes and discovered that my desk was covered with his debris. I became enraged. Part of me told me to leave the room and to come back when I was calmer. But I stayed and exploded. The flood of abuse poured out of my mouth. I was out of control. Every mean thought I had ever harbored about him escaped from the inner recesses of my mind. "Fat," "cheap," "gross," "selfish" and "dumb" were some of the lighter insults I delivered. When I finished with my tirade, I remember him looking at me unbelieving. He said nothing. He just turned and walked away. We never spoke again. I found another roommate. And I lost a friend that I wanted to keep. After my rage had been spent, I desired with all my heart, to take back the words that I had uttered. But it was too late.

Since that time, I fear my anger. I have no desire to lose my *cool*. My *cool* is the defense of my best interests and the welfare of the people I love. When I feel enraged, I walk away. I refuse to confront people when I am uncontrollably angry. My reason and my anger have different agendas. It is dangerous to turn my life over to rage. I walk away until I can return calmer, until I can see the consequences of my action. I am not interested in rituals of forgiveness. They are generally insincere. People do not easily forget insults even when they claim to forgive.

Constructive *cool* is an important part of sanity. It balances defiance and kindness. It balances reason and emotion. It balances realism and truthfulness. When we are realistic we do not hide from the facts. One of the facts is that human egos are very fragile, that people have a hard time facing facts. Another fact is that we are people too.

LAUGHTER

One summer in my youth I served as a bellhop on a summer pleasure boat that plied the waters of the Great Lakes. It travelled every week from Buffalo to Duluth and back. The passengers were either older couples looking for a quiet restful holiday—or, strangely enough, young women looking for social opportunities. Unfortunately, very few single men chose the voyage. Bellhops and busboys had to cushion the frustration.

One Saturday afternoon we were receiving passengers from Buffalo. It seemed as though three hundred eager secretaries had naively signed up for the trip. One of the new passengers was this enormously fat woman who had trouble maneuvering the gangplank. Folds of skin covered her exposed arms and legs. But her face was quite wonderful, with a kind of intelligent and mischievous smile. One of the other bellhops, a handsome young man, took her baggage to the room. It was the beginning of "fatal attraction."

For the next week my poor friend was pursued by this eager woman around the decks of the ship. Since she wasn't romantically interested in me, we had several long quiet conversations. She was a mathematics teacher in high school, very bright and very good-humored. She was enjoying the chase.

On the Friday evening before we returned to Buffalo, she spied my friend on the deck. She half ran toward him. He saw her and dashed down a narrow stairway to the galley. She followed, without checking the width of the stairs. Disaster ensued. She got wedged in the stairwell, her thighs imprisoned by two metal walls. I was in the galley when I heard the commotion outside. I ran up the stairs and confronted her. She looked angry and humiliated. Everybody had gathered on the deck above her and were staring.

And then—all of a sudden—she looked at me and she burst out laughing. "Shit," she said, "this is grotesque." And then she laughed some more.

Life has an absurdity to it. It sometimes traps us in existential stairwells with no exit. We cannot figure out why we are there. And we cannot change what has happened. There are three alternatives. We can resign ourselves piously to the situation and pray, knowing that in some mysterious way getting stuck in a stairwell is for our own good. We can cry, wail and scream, hoping that some rescue force will hear our cry, take pity on us, and save us. Or we can laugh.

Laughter is neither friendly nor reverent nor resigned. In the story of evolution it started out as turned away anger. Displaying teeth is not usually a friendly gesture. It is a prelude to biting. But instead of biting laughers open their mouths and howl. There is always an edge of hostility to laughing. "Biting" humor and mockery are always on the edge of even the kindest joke. When we hear laughter we are never sure whether they are laughing with us or at us.

Traditional religion and laughter are opposite ways of responding to the human condition. The heart of religion is worship, a recurrent surrender to the will of God. Worship rests on the profound conviction that all is well with the world even though the world appears to be sick. God is loving, just and orderly even though we do not seem to be experiencing a lot of love, justice and moral order. From the human perspective the world is crazy. From the divine perspective the world, with all its supernatural rewards and punishments, is a wonderful place.

Laughing starts with the absurdity of life. Life is frustrating. The world is not fair. The good are punished more than they ought to be. The wicked are rewarded more than they ought to be. Kindness gets you rejection. Cruelty gets you power. Laughter is rarely welcome in religious institutions.

Laughter is a safe expression of anger and discomfort with the way life goes. It helps to drain our anger and keeps us from both apoplexy and going crazy.

Realists love laughter. It is one of their best strategies for survival. They resist resignation and avoid waiting. When the absurdity of the universe traps them in the stairwell, they throw their heads back and laugh.

12

CONSTRUCTIVE LOVE
Step 7

Everybody loves love. It is humanity's favorite emotion. Many people are uncomfortable with fear and with anger. But nobody is publicly uncomfortable with love. People want to be loved. They also want other people to think that they are loving.

The romance of love is everywhere. Some people believe that love is the essence of the universe, that love conquers all. Others believe that love is the foundation of morality, that all things done in the name of love are right. It is the general human consensus that the more love there is the better world there will be.

Romancing love, however, is a problem. Something that everybody favors turns into a cliche. If all people want to be loving, then they will be tempted to define whatever they do as love. *Love*, like *democracy*, becomes a catchword for a million different kinds of feelings and actions, many of them wildly different one from the other. What unites them is a word that everybody wants to claim.

Parents who beat their children often say that they do it out of love. Politicians who repress their citizens often claim to love the people. Religious leaders who demand conformity often call it the love of God. If you want to "justify" any action you call it love.

So what is love? And why is it important for sanity?

Love began millions of years ago. Fear and anger were old when love began. Love emerged because flight and confrontation were no longer enough to guarantee survival. Birds and mammals produced vulnerable young who needed to be fed and cared for before they matured. The "babies" were too weak to fend for themselves. They needed to share space with their protective parents. They needed to turn off the old triggers of fear and anger and find a warm spot next to their mother and father.

Love began with loving children. All other forms of love are derivatives. The first love experience is the love of our mother. The quality of that love will determine who and what we are and how we ultimately express our own love. The child at the mother's breast is the opening scene of love. And, in some way, that scene remains with us to the end of our lives. Since our infancy is so long, since we take so many more years to grow up than our evolutionary cousins, there is a part of us that always remains the child, a part of us that always yearns for the comforts of that moment at the breast.

The love of men for women grew out of the love of children. Vulnerable children meant vulnerable women. And vulnerable women required the support of protective men. Men and women bonded in order to raise children. Erotic love was the support system of basic love. The family was born. Parents and children began to do what nature had formerly abhorred. They stuck together in the same space. Sometimes they argued and fought because sharing space was new and not easy. But they generally stayed together. The power of love overcame the counter-power of fear and anger. As little infants we are intruders. Love turns us into cuddly babies and makes it possible for us to grow up.

The love of friends comes from the same place. Vulnerable families needed support against a harsh and unrelenting nature. Families banded together. Communities emerged. Men bonded to hunt for food together. Friendships began. Fraternal love joined erotic love. In time, women who tended the hearth, found their own connections with other women. Fraternal love is rarely as strong as erotic love. And erotic love, despite its fleshiness pales before the power of mother love.

Love is confusing. Sometimes we forget what play we are playing in. Husbands want their wives to be their mothers. Wives want their husbands to be their fathers. Needy friends insist that we become their parents. Under the surface of so much love is the attachment and dependency of childhood. If people were independent and self-sufficient love would not be necessary. Only in Ayn Rand fantasies, or in the cliched hype of the new self-esteem psychology, do men and women come together for no other reason than mutual attraction. Nurturing and being nurtured have more complex roots.

Love produces its own ambivalence. Sometimes attachment and dependency smother us. We want our own space. We want our own dignity. We want to be individuals. When we are teenagers growing up we discover the power of anger. Anger drives our parents away. Anger makes us separate. But separation makes us afraid. Our rebellion is only half-hearted. We still need and want our parents. And so the dance of life begins. Love and anger tango with each other. When we feel vulnerable and alone we want love. When we feel strong and self-sufficient we want dignity. Balancing love and anger is never easy.

Like all emotions love is more than an internal feeling. It is also an external behavior. The critical sign of love is nurturing—feeding, sheltering, protecting, stroking. Sexual passion is not love, unless it is accompanied by caring attachment. If you love somebody, you desire to do more than adore them. You are sensitive to their needs and want to satisfy them. There is a part of all love that is parental and supportive. There are many illusions about love. Some imagine that love, and love alone, is sufficient for life. They regard hate, envy, fear and anger as purely negative emotions, wicked anti-social drives that only love can dispel. They fail to acknowledge that love is only one of many survival strategies. There are times when love does not arrange for happiness. There are times when hate and anger are more appropriate. Loving Adolph Hitler would not have saved humanity from the scourge of fascism.

Others imagine that love arises spontaneously. It cannot be planned or cultivated. It is some kind of magical, ethereal, spiritual substance that has very little to do with ordinary feeling and ordinary behavior. They fail to observe that most loving relationships have no magic to them. They are maintained by routine and consistent caring. Often, as in arranged marriages, the behavior of love provides the feeling of love. People grow attached to what they choose to nurture. While their fantasy love conjures up images of compelling attractiveness, their real love is a person they nurture and take for granted. Only the absence or death of this individual makes them realize how much they loved them.

Still others maintain that it is not possible to love others unless you first love yourself. This is one of the cliches of modern popular psychology, the claim that self-love comes first. The result of this illusion is the behavioral self-hypnosis that has become so much a part of self-esteem therapy. Millions of people spend millions of hours telling themselves that they are lovable and worthy of happiness. One devotee of "self-esteem" told me that "she now just loves herself to death"—although there is nothing about her behavior to indicate that she does. True self-esteem—which is a sense of strength and empowerment—cannot come from flattering yourself. Mantras of "I just love myself" are about as substantial as air in a balloon. Empowerment comes from doing things "powerful" and having other people recognize your achievement. Strength comes from trying to be strong and succeeding. Self-love is the child of love. First we receive the love of parents. If we did not have loving parents, then simply telling ourselves that we are lovable does not work. Only when we discover that we can nurture others and, in turn, receive the love and approval of people other than our mother and father, does genuine self-love emerge.

"Wounded children" are not healed by dwelling on their wounds in an orgy of self-pity and then defiantly proclaiming that they are lovable. Since we are all vulnerable, fragile social beings, in need of the approval of others, healing the wounds inflicted by callous parents comes from finding alternative people to love us and respect us. But they will not do that in any meaningful way unless we earn that approval by what we do. Self-love arises for the wounded in the same way it arises for the non-wounded. Fortunate infants receive the love of parents and then come to love themselves. Along the way they learn how to please others and their self-love is reinforced by more approval. Unfortunate infants do not receive the love of parents. They have difficulty pleasing others, even the people they love and respect. But they cannot be healed by pretending that they do not need the love of others. Since they are no longer infants, looking helpless and needy only earns them pity, not respect. There is nothing wrong with self-flattery. But it is never enough. Acting worthy usually precedes feeling worthy. Verbal self-loving is no substitute for competence.

Henry was a "wounded child." His father was an abusive alcoholic; his mother a whining self-absorbed woman incapable of any sustained nurturing. He grew up ashamed and fearful and hungry for love and approval. He was a moody unattractive boy, a schoolbook drudge who always assumed that he was going to be rejected. Working his way through college he became a workaholic accountant (a response to his undisciplined father), but was never very successful in his work. There was something too depressing about him to win over clients. One day he encountered self-esteem therapy. He discovered that he was angry and resentful over all the hurt that he had suffered as a child. He felt cheated of the love and nurturing that other children had received and he had not. But he was determined to love himself now and to change his life. There was a kind of comic bravado to his new assertiveness. But there was no visible change in his depression, posture and responses. He thought he was different. Two years after he began his therapy he abandoned it. Shortly after, he met a young woman who was kind and patient and eager for marriage. She encouraged him to have more fun, to dress differently, to stand up straight. He was reluctant to make the change at first. But when he saw how people responded to him more positively he persisted. He became more relaxed, more desirous, more attractive to others. He stopped complaining about his abusive parents, an enormous relief to the people who wanted to like him but had been turned off by his self-pity. He also began to nurture his lover and felt more self-confident. And he stopped telling people he liked himself because he really did.

There is no doubt about it. There are many illusions about love. That is why it often drives us crazy. We are not quite sure what it is. And we do not know what to do with its power. The *grand illusion* imagines that the universe loves us. The *love illusion* imagines that love exists for its own sake—unrestricted by any alternatives and indifferent to any consequences.

Realistic love rejects these illusions. It tries to live with the truth.

FALLING IN LOVE MAY NOT BE LOVE

Erotic and romantic love is the favorite theme of most popular stories. Mother and father stories warm our hearts. Friendship stories can be uplifting. But romantic tales grab us with the power of sexual intensity. The best part of the story is when two people fall in love and experience the euphoria and ecstasy of the first encounters.

But falling in love may be a deceptive beginning to the real thing. When people fall in love they often fantasize about who and what their love is. They often see things that are not there. They often see things that they want and need to see. Lovers at this stage become illusions. They are the projections of each other's imagination. If we are weak we want our lover to be strong. If we are awkward, we want out lover to be graceful. If we are afraid we want our lover to be brave.

Our lovers complete us because we feel incomplete. Together we become one ideal person.

With such "romantic hype" disappointment is inevitable. It happens frequently. The balloon bursts and we confront the reality of our partner. Some of us get angry and depart. Some of us stay, mourn and get depressed. Others adjust their vision and move from falling in love to love.

Hank was a hopeless romantic. Facts annoyed him because they interfered with his vision of the world. He was always going away on exotic vacations, hoping to meet the exotic and different woman of his dreams. The "girls" back in Detroit reminded him too much of his mother and sisters. He loved them, but he found them too ordinary to be role models for marriage. On a Club Med trip to Tahiti he met Felice. She was a shapely brunette from Paris who spoke English with an irresistible French accent. Hank was swept away with passion. He proposed marriage after three days. She resisted. But her resistance made her even more attractive. He persisted. She yielded. She came to Detroit. Hank married her. Felice was ordinary. She was a high school graduate from Lille who sold perfume to tourists on the Place Vendome. She was pleasant and loving but not Brigitte Bardot. Six months after the wedding Hank left Felice. He told his friends that Felice was not the woman he thought she was, that he had fallen out of love, and that he wanted a divorce. The problem was that Felice said that she still loved him and that she wanted to make the marriage work. He saw no point in continuing the relationship. The excitement was gone for him. Since then he has married two times. Both marriages failed. Both marriages, like the one to Felice, were to two women he met on "exotic" vacations.

Deborah was also romantic, just like Hank. She grew up loving the movies and the heroes of the screen. Robert Taylor was gone but Robert Redford was there and available for her in the darkness of the theater. As a child, she hated to leave the cinema palace to return home. Ordinary life seemed to have people who were too short, too fat, too afraid and too awkward. When she grew up and became a lawyer her romantic vision never left her. On a blind date she met Steve and fell in love. Steve looked and talked like Robert Redford. He was the WASP dream for a suburban Jewish over-achiever, who was not exactly sure that she was attractive. He returned her passion. Six months of ecstasy followed. A small wedding to accommodate uncomfortable parents was followed by a euphoric honeymoon to the Greek isles. Even defecating donkeys on Santorini could not undermine the image of perfection. But coming home and settling down turned into a painful disappointment. Steve was a gym teacher with a limited salary. He was not as ambitious as Deborah or as intellectual. He was very athletic and she was not. She preferred concerts to ball games. His parents were friendly but bland. Her parents were hoping that the marriage would end. She became very depressed. She thought of terminating the marriage. But she did not. She was afraid of her fantasies. She was afraid that the divorce would be followed by another marriage, another illusion, another divorce. Plus she loved Steve, not in the way she had before, but through more realistic eyes. She found comfort in the way they nurtured each other even though they often disagreed. He was no longer her savior, her prince of beauty. But he was strong, kind, funny and loving. The euphoria was gone. There would always be some disappointment. But the relationship worked. He was no longer the answer to all her deficiencies. Yet his skills and personality complemented hers. They were a good team.

Hank was never interested in love. Unlike Deborah he was only interested in falling in love. Love is reaching out, nurturing, giving support. Its value is not only in the magic of the lover, but also in the bonds of dependency that come from mutual help. Falling in love is self-absorbed and slightly desperate. The role of the lover is to play a part in a movie that has been scripted by the deficiencies of her partner. She is to be what he wants to be but cannot.

Falling in love may be one of the possible beginnings to authentic love. But it presents a formidable problem. In an age when love relationships can be so easily entered into and left, few social pressures exist to encourage lovers to go beyond falling in love to love. How does one know that beyond the fantasy there may exist something worthwhile? After all, authentic love is also romantic, even though it is good-humored.

BEING JUDGMENTAL

Someone told me recently that her second marriage was so much better than her first. Her first husband had been very judgmental and demanding. She always felt that she was on trial with him. Her new husband was non-judgmental and accepting. He loved her for what she was, not for what he wanted her to be. "If only," she sighed, "people could be more accepting and less judgmental. There would be so much more love in the world."

Her sentiments were echoed by a young student who was complaining to me about his parents. He told me that their love for him was a sham. They had never accepted his decision to leave the university and to live modestly in Ann Arbor while writing poetry during the day and playing his guitar at night. They were always telling him what he was doing wrong. Even when they gave him money to pay his expenses their gift was always accompanied by negative criticism. "Why can't people stop judging other people and just accept and love them for what they are?"

Being judgmental is now "out" in fashionable psychotherapeutic cures. Being non-judgmental is now "in." The worst thing you can do to people is not to accept them for what they are. If you truly love people, if you truly love them, you do not try to remake them according to your plan. You encourage them to live according to their plan. Putting people on trial is an act of cruelty. Making demands is an inappropriate art of intrusion. True love is a paradise of mutual acceptance.

When George returned from his trip of self-discovery to India and Nepal, he told his wife that his life had completely changed and that now he wanted to pursue his personal enlightenment. Although he was a successful obstetrician and was the father of three small sons, he felt compelled to return to India for a year to continue his self-exploration. She would have to fend for herself until he returned. But he hoped that she would understand how important this search for personal enlightenment was to him and would accept who and what he had become. He said that he loved her and the children very much and that they were always in his thoughts wherever he went. When his wife protested and screamed that she could not understand how this abandonment was an act of love, he countered calmly by assuring her that if she truly loved him she would not sit in judgment. She would allow him to do what he had to do. The distraught wife was beside herself. She had "foolishly" assumed that love was more than accepting the unacceptable.

In the late sixties the Fritz Perls view of ideal human relations emerged. Two individuals encounter each other. They are attracted to each other. They decide to be together. They are mutually self-affirming. "I am not in this world to serve you. You are not in this world to serve me. I am I. You are you. As long as it is satisfying to be together let us be together. Let us not seek to change each other but to accept and love each other. And when the relationship is no longer satisfying let us part as friends." No judgment and no demands. We are above jealousy, anger, resentment and inappropriate expectations.

If this is love, who needs hate? Love is not doing what you want to do and having your lover say "OK." Love is not dumping your personal garbage on the head of your lover and having your lover say, "Thank you."

There is a difference between hateful judgment and loving judgment. Hateful judgment is indifferent to your welfare and happiness. It is indifferent to the moral consequences of your actions. It is tied up with the vested interest of the judge. Hateful judges often pose as loving judges. They are always talking about "your welfare" and "your duty." But they do not mean it. They really want to use you for their agenda.

Ann did not discover that she was a lesbian until she finished medical school. She had resisted her feelings for so long. But in her first year of residency she met Barbara and they discovered that they loved each other. Barbara was also a physician in her last year of a surgical residency. She came from a very religious fundamentalist family that severed their connection with her when she told them about her life style. Ann and Barbara set up house together. Ann was uncomfortable initially with the arrangement, but soon she became more open about the relationship. Her parents were unaware of what was happening in Ann's life until they came to visit Ann and discovered Barbara. Ann's parents thought of themselves as liberals. Her father was a successful and wealthy lawyer. They had many prominent friends. When Ann told them about her new life style, they were shocked and unaccepting. They scolded Ann. They pleaded with her to leave Barbara. Their response seemed inconsistent with so many of the liberal stands they had taken in the past. Ann suspected that they were not very concerned with her happiness. They were afraid of what their friends and colleagues would say once the word about Ann's new life style would pass through the rumor mill and reach home. They told Ann that they could not accept her new life—and that if she persisted in being with Barbara they would have nothing more to do with her. They told her that they loved her—because of that, they could not stand by and let her destroy her life. Ann was devastated by their judgment. Their pride in her success had been a very important part of her own self-esteem. She was crushed by their rejection. She saw herself as a good person who had committed herself to a loving relationship and to the work of healing sick people. How could her parents have been so cruel?

And it was cruel. It had nothing to do with conscience or the welfare of Ann. It was based on the fear of public opinion. It was a hateful judgment.

Larry was an only son, the "apple" of his unloved mother's eye. She had worked very hard as an underpaid librarian to put her son through the university and law school. Larry was a brilliant student, whose analytic mind was praised by his teachers and fellow students. In his final year of law school he met Fay, a waitress in a local restaurant. Fay was a university dropout, a drug user, and a conscientious defier of convention. She hated authority; she hated straight society; she cultivated an air of weary hedonism. She was also very attractive and very charismatic. Larry was drawn to Fay and her sexy cynicism. He fell in love. She returned his ardor. She poked fun at his conventional ambitions. She talked about a life style that would be free of the "stupid conformities" of bourgeois society. She urged him to leave law school and to join her in a new and exciting counterculture journey through Mexico. He wrote his mother and told her that he was dropping out of law school and traveling with Fay. He asked her to understand that he was doing this after a thoughtful reflection on his life and on what was important for his happiness. He said that he knew that she would accept his decision because she loved him. But she did not accept his decision. She went up to Ann Arbor to see him. She confronted him. She told him that he was throwing away his life and his ambition for something so vague that he himself could not describe it. Larry told her that his life was his life and that he was free to do with it as he wanted. She refused to relent. She left him with her passionate disapproval. Her judgment was harsh but loving.

Love is nurturing. Because it is nurturing it is also demanding. Children make demands on parents. Parents make demands on children. Spouses make demands on each other. Only in never-never land do lovers offer total acceptance to lovers.

CONDITIONAL LOVE

"Unconditional love" is very popular. For many people love is only real when it is unconditional. Unconditional love is sacrificial love. It says that, no matter what you do to me, I will continue to nurture you. Sacrificial love is the love that martyrs love. I am prepared to give up my possessions and even my life, for you, because love is my ultimate value. There is no higher value. Love exists for its own sake. For some *unconditionalists* love is the very essence of God, the very glue that holds the universe together.

The implications of unconditional love are clear. No matter what you choose to say and do I will never abandon you. Your behavior is irrelevant to my commitment. I love you not because of you but because of love. As my supreme value, love prevails. Even your rotten and intolerable behavior cannot persuade me to abandon my commitment to love. No matter how hard you try to make me angry and reject you, I will not reject you. No matter how hard you try to look pitiable and win my sympathy, I will always respond to your desperation with love.

Realistic people value love. But they do not value unconditional love. It does not make any sense to them. It appears to be nothing more than a form of irrational masochism. Love is very important for happiness and survival. But it cannot be the supreme value. When abusive and destructive people threaten the happiness and survival of both individuals and communities, they cannot be loved without violating values more important than love. Love, at the price of self-destruction, is a form of insanity. It adds personal craziness to the craziness of the universe.

When I was a child, I lived on a street where the houses were close together. On a summer's night, with all the windows open, you could hear the ordinary and extraordinary noises of family living. From time to time you could hear hollering and screaming. Domestic arguments were part of the local drama. On my street there was an odd family. The husband worked in the motor building of the Ford Rouge plant. His job was repetitious drudgery and he would arrive home dirty and tired. His wife was a seamstress, quiet and industrious and very withdrawn. They kept very much to themselves. Even their daughter, who was in my class at school, was afraid to talk to anybody. Some summer evenings loud screams would come through their windows and pierce the summer quiet. The man was beating his wife. You could almost hear the whack of his hand against her body. The daughter would run out of the house, put her hands over her ears and start to cry. We were all transfixed, not quite knowing what to do but to listen to the sound of the violence. No one intervened. The beating would stop. The next day the wife would appear with swollen eyes and swollen lips.

One day I was in the local grocery shop with my mother. The wife was buying butter. One of my neighbors walked up to her and very boldly asked her why she did not leave her husband. The woman did not seem to be embarrassed by the question. Without hesitating—

and with tears coming into her eyes—she said very simply, "You see, I love my husband very much." Although I was only eight years old, I remember being puzzled at her reply. I could not understand how you could love somebody who beat you into a bloody pulp. I had expected some answer like, "Where would I go. I have no money." But I was unaware of the power of unconditional love. Now— having witnessed many years of the human drama—I am no longer surprised. Masochism is universal. And its rationalization is the love that has no limits.

Rational people love love. But they do not love love absolutely. There are limits and boundaries to love. They are willing to give. They are willing to give more than they receive. But they are not willing to exchange love for hatred and cruelty. They are not prepared to be sacrificial lambs on the altar of unconditional acceptance.

When the daughter of the abused woman grew up she married a friend of mine, a man who had gone to school with both of us. I feared for her. My friend was violent and very abusive. I imagined that she had unconsciously chosen somebody just like her father—and that she would imitate the masochism of her mother. But, strangely enough, she responded very differently. After an initial outburst of violence she moved out of the house for a month. When she returned, her husband was repentant and begged her forgiveness. But soon after, a trivial quarrel about lost car keys escalated into a scene of uncontrollable rage. He attacked her. She fled. She never returned. She sued for divorce.

The act of leaving her husband seemed to liberate her. It gave her a sense of control over her life that she had never known before. She became more open and gregarious. When I met her at our high school reunion the awkward withdrawal had been replaced by a welcome smile. She was very willing to talk about her marriage and about the deep attachment she had felt for her husband. But her memory of her mother's humiliation prevented her from repeating her mother's story. "I said to myself—if this is the reward for loving my husband, then there is something wrong with my love."

Love is sometimes bad. It is sometimes self-destructive. It is sometimes the unwilling ally of our deeds. When it is good it can be wonderful. When it is bad it is no different from self-destructive fear or self-destructive anger. Choosing healthy love means setting the limits.

MANY ROLES

Love requires imagination. It requires us to play many parts in many dramas. If we are humorless, we refuse to play more than one part. We insist that there is only way to be loving.

When we feel strong and self-confident we want our lovers to be our equals, nurturing friends who do not smother us with affection. But when we feel needy and dependent, we want our lovers to be our parents, mothering and fathering us in our hour of weakness.

Humorless people cannot tolerate weakness. They abolish it from "acceptable" love relationships. They insist that spouse love and friendship love should be based on self-esteeming equality. They insist that playing the parent is a violation of adult dignity. If we are searching for mothers and fathers we will abuse our lovers.

Moments of weakness are as much a part of the human condition as moments of strength. We cannot legislate human needs. They simply are what they are. It is an act of cruelty to tell them that they have to be something else. All that happens from this demand is that needy people pretend to be strong and are too embarrassed to ask for the love that they require.

Sander lost his job on his birthday. He was a middle exec-utive in a failing computer service firm. He was expecting advancement. Instead he got fired. When he returned home to tell his wife what had happened, he began to cry. He had never cried before in her presence. She had always seen him as this strong self-reliant friend. His uncontrolled despair frightened her. She saw him becoming a helpless child before her very eyes. She had no desire to be his mother. She loved him because he was her best friend and equal. His loss of nerve unnerved her. She did not know how to respond. She lectured him on being strong. She never thought of putting her arms around him and holding him. She did not want her husband to be a baby.

But sometimes even the strongest of adults feel like babies. They feel vulnerable and needy. They need mother love as much as they need lectures on self-esteem. If they can only be children for a short while they will recover their strength and return to the role of friend and equal. Sensitive and caring lovers do not mind playing par-ent when the circumstances demand. They are prepared to nurture their partners in whatever way they need to be nurtured.

The drama of love requires us to play many parts. Sometimes we are the admiring audience. Sometimes we are the challenging friend. Sometimes we are the fun companion. Sometimes we are the protective parent. No single role is superior to another. Each is a response to the needs of our lover. Most successful relationships depend on this repertory of skills. Inflexibility narrows the possibility of love.

Sander's marriage did not survive the loss of his job. His wife could not accept his temporary weakness. She could not deal with his neediness. She was a one-role player. Mothering was not her cup of tea. Sander turned to his friends. Philip was a bachelor acquaintance from business school. He offered Sander hospitality and shelter. He made no demands on him for a while. Within two weeks Sander's sadness lifted. He stopped mourning his job. He felt stronger. He began the search for new work.

Good friends and good lovers do not invent the human condition. They live with it. They do not exaggerate their own strength and they are not embarrassed by their weakness. They know that if God exists, he does not need love. He is always strong and self-sufficient. Humans crave love because they are needy and dependent. If they are less needy they can play the equal. If they are more needy they might play the child. Realistic people can play the part that love demands.

13

RATIONAL GUILT
Step 6

GUILT IS NO LONGER FASHIONABLE. In "liberated" circles it has been the enemy for the past ninety years. No crime is worse than subjecting a fellow human being to a "guilt trip." Guilt dispensers are regarded as "liberty poopers," happiness subverters, self-righteous moral intruders.

Erasing the harmful effects of guilt has been one of the major tasks of psychotherapy. Freeing people from sexual repression, gender repression, work repression, family repression has become almost a crusade on the part of many freedom-minded psychologists and psychiatrists. To be free of oppressive and unnecessary guilt is to be healthy. Guilt removal is regarded by many as the path to sanity.

Irrational rules have produced "irrational" suffering. People deserve relief from this useless pain.

The assault on guilt is a passionate response to a world where guilt reigned supreme. In the world of traditional religion sin was an obsession. Almost any desire or pleasure had sinful possibilities. The safest way to live was to resist desire and to avoid pleasure. Since bodily lusts are hard to dismiss, people walked around in a perpetual state of guilt. Only confession and priestly absolution provided any form of relief.

The Freudian revolution was a rebellion against this cruel regime. Sexual desire became normal. Repressing it became dangerous. Sin turned into a religious villain, draining all the legitimate fun and spontaneity from life. Guilt became sin's accomplice, paralyzing the will and filling human existence with useless anxiety. Fighting guilt became a holy psychotherapeutic crusade, especially since traditional religion was a powerful and formidable foe.

Guilt turned into a dirty word. It became a symbol of psychic repression. As individual freedom increased in an affluent consumer culture, choice replaced conformity as the norm of behavior. What you wanted might not be what I wanted. What was good for you might not be what was good for me. Sin became merely a personal preference. Life was transformed into life style. Duty ended up only as a "moral option."

Feeling guilty was now an embarrassment. It was a sign of mental disturbance, a sure indication that you were unable to accept your true feelings and desires. Transcending guilt was now the goal of mentally healthy people. Healthy people never tried to impose their moral standards on others. They lived and let live. They found no significant place for guilt in their lives. Morality was a personal choice.

Understanding, tolerance and self-acceptance were to replace the tyranny of the old shame.

> Ralph chose eight years of intense psychoanalysis. Coming from a very religious and fundamentalist Lutheran background he had grown up feeling guilty about his sexual desire. His repression had been so severe that even masturbation had filled him with uncontrollable shame. When he first married, he discovered that he was impotent. This humiliation brought him to an analyst and to a journey of self-discovery. His "liberation" from guilt turned his conversation into missionary zeal. He now denounced religion and the terrible regime of repression which he had endured. Guilt was the enemy and had to be resisted at all costs. When he was challenged by others and reminded that sexual guilt was not the only guilt around, he was unresponsive. His sexual journey was so painful that all other forms of guilt were simply dumped into the same psychic garbage pit.

The battle against irrational guilt turned irrationally into the battle against guilt. The pendulum of educated public opinion swung from one extreme to another. "Guilt trip" was now bad no matter what the guilt. If you were a "flake" and never kept your promises, who was your neighbor to tell you how to live and how to handle your commitments? If you were smart and lazy and never disciplined your potential, who was your mother to make you feel bad about your life style decision? If you were self-absorbed and hedonistic, who was your friend to denounce your lack of concern for the welfare of others? An odd emotional logic emerged. Repressing masturbation was bad; therefore, repressing "flakiness" was bad.

Inappropriate guilt turned appropriate guilt into an enemy by association.

Guilt is a perfectly normal emotion. Like all human emotions that have survived the test of evolution, it has its place in the human repertory of useful feelings. We human beings are "social animals." We are not loners. We cannot survive in isolation. We need the support and nurturing of other people. Even when we grow up we are still dependent on the protection of others. Guilt, like love, is the glue that keeps groups together and functioning. Its power is innate. Its style is cooperation and sharing. Guilt works where love fails. It tames reluctant members of the community whose nurturing instincts may be limited. Where love has no appeal, duty may.

Since guilt emerged later than fear, anger and love it is often weaker than they are. People who are very afraid or very angry or very lustful are driven to do what guilt resists. Even people who are tortured by guilt frequently do what their conscience forbids. They cannot control their behavior. And they cannot control their feelings. They are helpless to be what they want to be. But they cannot change what they do.

Many psychologists maintain that guilt is not an original instinctive feeling. They say that it is an acquired emotion. Freud maintained that guilt is fear. As infants we are punished for anti-social behavior. We are afraid of the punishment and want to avoid it. In time that fear is internalized and becomes guilt. Guilt is only a variation on fear. It is molded by social circumstance and conditioning. If we could avoid the influence of family and society we would never feel guilty.

Now there is no doubt that what people feel guilty about varies from society to society and that reality might be evidence that guilt is acquired rather than innate. Cannibals in cannibal society do not feel guilty about eating people. Warriors in warlike societies do not feel guilty about impaling enemies. But, then, the same variation occurs in what arouses people's love or fear or anger. In a feudal world bowing and scraping keeps superiors from getting angry. In an urban, egalitarian world few bosses expect bowing and scraping and even fewer would get angry if their employees refused to do it. In a matriarchal society men love and nurture their sister's children rather than their own natural offspring. In a patriarchal society they love and nurture their own. The capacity for guilt is like the capacity for love, fear or anger. There is a general context in which the feelings are aroused. The specifics sometimes vary from culture to culture. Yet many of the specifics are also the same. Feeling guilty about betraying friends and comrades is universal.

The refusal to allow guilt to be an intrinsic and innate human feeling is part of the silly campaign against guilt. If guilt is socially acquired, then it can be eliminated. If a community is sufficiently permissive then guilt will vanish. A guiltless world becomes a utopian vision based on reality. The problem is that what pretends to be a utopian reality is really a utopian fantasy. The origins of guilt do not lie only in social conditioning. They lie mainly in human nature.

People vary in their capacity for guilt just as they vary in their capacity for love. People who are disposed to too much guilt become either too fearful or too ascetic. Men and women who have no capacity for guilt are emotional defectives and become sociopaths. Those who have a normal disposition find personal satisfaction in ethical activity and work constructively to improve the welfare of their family and community. People without guilt are people without conscience.

The dynamics of guilt is the opposite of personal autonomy and assertiveness. It is the ability and need to identify with "something greater than myself." That something is no otherworldly spirit. It is the worldly community which gives me life and helps me to survive. The first experience of transcendence is not spiritual. It is ethical. It is a sense of deep attachment to and deep dependence on the family which bore me and nurtured me. Clans, tribes and nations are extensions of my family and often evoke the same loyalty. I cannot betray them by my action and find that feeling guiltless is easy. It is unrealistic to assume that our family connections are trivial. Guilt is the internal discomfort I feel when I violate the welfare of my group. It shrinks my self-esteem and makes me feel smaller in my own eyes.

Guilt is easiest to invoke when the community we serve looks like us and our family. After all, guilt evolved in a world where groups were small and where its members were genetically related. The modern world of large states and multi-ethnic nations is a different world for guilt to operate in. Whites have trouble identifying with blacks. Blacks have trouble identifying with Asians. Our coming together is too recent for evolution to have had the time to improve guilt. The fear and hatred of strangers is an old fear. It often accompanied an intense loyalty to our own group. Historic guilt has trouble transcending that barrier even when it needs to. Transcendence is very selective about what it is willing to include in its outreach. The man who is prepared to die for his own child is often just as prepared to kill the child of the stranger.

One of the most familiar movie scripts of my childhood involved the brutal gangster who showed no mercy to his enemies or to innocent strangers. He was cruel and destructive above and beyond what any modern morality could sustain. Yet he had a widowed mother and a little daughter whom he adored. He was loving and gentle with them. He would give them anything that they wanted. He would even sacrifice his own life to make sure that no harm came to them. He was a "good guy," but only to a small and selective group of people.

Guilt is not love. Love is intimate nurturing. Guilt may encourage love. But it does not begin with love. It begins with who and what I feel I am. If I feel myself only as an individual, then guilt has no place in my life. If I feel myself as a member of my family, and only as a member of my family, then guilt operates very narrowly in my existence. But if I feel myself part of something greater than my family and can sustain this feeling, then guilt can lead even to the embracing of strangers. In some strange way strangers can also become 'family.' Empathy turns into sympathy. Their pain becomes my pain. Their pleasure becomes my pleasure.

Guilt can operate even where there is no love. I do not have to love people in order to avoid harming them. I do not have to love people in order to help them. Love is an intense nurturing, so intense that it is impossible to love more than a few people. When someone says to me that he loves everybody, I cringe at the exaggeration. It is impossible to love everybody. Love requires intimacy. Guilt does not. Guilt, not love, makes me respect your dignity. Guilt, not love, makes me help you satisfy your needs. Guilt, not love, makes me offer you protection even when you are not lovable.

Duty is a word with a famous past. But it has fallen out of fashion in a world that finds guilt distasteful. Yet, there is no other word that can take its place, that can convey its unique meaning. Duty flows from obligation. Obligation comes from mutual dependency. Mutual dependency makes us feel tied to one another. Boundaries blur and we come to find our strength and our identity, not only in ourselves, but also in the group to which we belong. Betraying the group is like betraying ourselves. If we identify too much with the group we will lose our sense of control over our own lives and forego our happiness and dignity. But if we identify too little with the group, we feel alone and weak and sometimes lose our self-esteem. There is an irony to self-esteem. The enthusiasm and approval of others in a shared cause give us strength. If we never experience that strength, we will never be able to resist the group when it misbehaves, when it chooses a course of self-destruction. Self-esteem, like ethics, is a balancing act between the individual and the group. The arbiter is rational guilt.

When I was ten years old, I spent the summer visiting relatives in New York. It was so different from my home town of Detroit. I loved the midtown skyscrapers, the endless blocks of apartment buildings, the crowds in the street on a hot summer's night. One afternoon my aunt took me to Radio City to see the Rockettes. While entering the theater a large woman in front of me tripped on a stair, fell forward, but caught herself before she hit the rug. While she lurched forward a ten dollar bill fell out of her hand and landed in front of my feet. She did not know that she had lost it. And nobody, not even my aunt, knew that I had found it, picked it up and quickly put it in my pocket. But only for a moment. A terrible wave of guilt assaulted me. I imagined myself losing ten dollars and having no one to return it. I saw my friends back home standing in a row and nodding their disapproval. I felt myself shrinking. The discomfort was unbearable. I reached into my pocket and ran after the woman and returned the ten dollars. She barely said thank you. But I did not care, I felt that I had done the right thing. It was as though I had made a promise to her that I had to keep.

Rational guilt is about keeping promises. It is about keeping promises that have never been formally made but which are just as real as a signed document. To live in society is to be part of an implied social contract. I will look out for you if you will look out for me. I will not do to you what I do not want you to do to me. Although we have never met, although we are strangers and have never directly helped each other, we share the human condition. We are both vulnerable and depend on the good will of others to survive. The act of living in the same world with you makes me dependent on you, as it makes you dependent on me. I never know when I will need you. And you never know when you will need me. This hypothetical dependency is a bond of solidarity and an implied promise. If I consent to live in society, I pledge, by implication, that, at least, I will not harm you.

Not harming you means that I will keep my promise to you, that I will not take from you what you have worked hard to possess, that I will not enhance my dignity at the price of yours, that I will never ask you to make sacrifices for me that are greater than what I am willing to make for you, that I will be trustworthy even where there is no fear of punishment, because a world without trust is worse than no world at all. Even if you do not keep your implied promise to me I will keep mine to you because what I do is done as much for the community we share as it is for you. Rational guilt rests on the realistic foundation that ethics is more than rational self-interest. Human nature makes us less individual and more collective than we are prepared to admit. Our social contract is based on the reality that my commitment to you may, in some way, reflect my commitment to me. This is no covenant between God and man. This is an understanding between people needing people. Realism finds no fault with guilt. It responds to it positively when the demands make sense. But when they do not it resists.

Edmund Burke, a British social philosopher, of the eighteenth century, spoke of this implied promise with passion: "Society is indeed a contract . . . It is to be looked on with . . . reverence, because it is not a partnership in things subservient only to the gross animal existence of a temporary and perishable nature. It is a partnership in all science; a partnership in all art; a partnership in every virtue, and in all perfection. As the ends of such a partnership cannot be obtained in many generations, it becomes a partnership not only between those who are living, but between those who are living, those who are dead, and those who are to be born." (*Reflections on the Revolution in France*)

Irrational guilt happens when guilt goes crazy and turns its energies to harm the people it exists to protect. Irrational guilt is not concerned with the realistic demands of the social contract. It assaults human nature and insists that it be different from what it is. It is uncomfortable with human desire and demands that it disappear. Trying to quench desire is a hard assignment. We can tame our feelings but we cannot dismiss them. Lust cannot be commanded to go away, nor can anger, nor can hate. Feeling guilty about what I am powerless to change is an enormous waste of time, a useless activity with no positive consequences, a reflection of the cruelty of so much religion and public opinion.

Irrational guilt, as Freud pointed out, must be unmasked for what it is and then dismissed. It stands in the way of human happiness and survival. Rational guilt, on the other hand, must be cultivated. It fine tunes the appropriate balance between the individual and the community. It is guided by our very powerful ideas.

BEHAVIOR

Patty hated her mother. It was sometimes difficult for her to talk civilly to this woman who bore her. From the moment of her birth Patty had been treated to invidious neglect. Her mother favored her older sister, who was prettier and more assertive than she was. As Patty grew up her mother would use her for menial work and reward her sister with material gifts and admiration. Patty put herself through accounting school, even though her mother had paid for her sister's failed education at a prestigious university. Shortly after qualifying as a certified public accountant, Patty married a fellow student. Her mother pled poverty and refused to pay for the wedding. Two years later Patty's sister moved to California and broke off communication with her mother and Patty. The distraught mother suffered a nervous breakdown and became increasingly dependent on Patty. Although Patty took care of her and supported her, her mother talked only about her sister. It was as though Patty did not exist. Patty cared for her mother out of a sense of duty, not out of love. She could not stop hating her, even though her mother was now pathetic. Patty felt guilty about her hate. She felt that daughters should love their mothers. She tried to drive the hate away. But it would not go away. No matter how hard she tried it insisted on its own presence. Her internal feeling of hostility rubbed up against her outer behavior of nurturing support. She could not stop feeling guilty. Her guilt tortured her.

Patty came to see me to find some relief. Maybe I could make her hate go away. I told Patty that she had no reason to feel guilty. She was a responsible person who took care of her mother. Her behavior was loving. Her behavior was something she could control. Her feelings were something she could not control. She could not be held responsible for what she could not control. Hate was a normal human response to rejection. It was not dangerous or immoral unless she acted on it. If her sister had remained to support her mother, Patty could have avoided her mother with no harmful consequences. But, under the circumstances, she had no choice. Duty does not require us to love the people we help. Rational guilt does not force us to like what we are obliged to support.

So many people worry about their feelings. So many people feel guilty about them. But, no matter how hard they try, they cannot drive them away. They insist on staying put, regardless of what their owners do. Many religions make an evil out of an "evil heart." They insist that people drive out "wicked" thoughts and "wicked" feelings from their conscious mind. But such a demand is itself immoral. Insisting that people change what they have no power to change is an act of cruelty. It is like insisting that blue-eyed people stop having blue eyes or that black people stop being black.

Realism does not give us impossible tasks. It only insists that we change what we have the power to change. Our behavior does not always conform to our internal feelings. And it is our behavior that counts. If I hate someone internally and can discipline myself to love them externally, that dichotomy is not "sin." It is virtue.

The counterpart to irrational guilt is irrational virtue. Irrational virtue means that my feelings count but my behavior does not. It is effortless ethics. If I have a good heart and rotten behavior, then my good heart is worthy of praise and my rotten behavior is excusable. How many times have we heard that meaningless complement "But he meant well." Meaning well is the only thing that makes a difference. Disciplining our behavior to conform to that noble intention is secondary.

A good heart has never helped anybody. A good heart attached to disciplined action is another story. We cannot help people with our good feelings. We can only help them with our good behavior. Rational guilt helps us see that difference.

If we persist in feeling guilty about feelings over which we have no control then we will hide from our feelings. Admitting what we feel is too hard to bear if it also makes us feel guilty. If anger, hate, lust and jealousy make us feel guilty, then we will pretend that we are not angry, that we do not hate, and that we are not lustful and jealous. And if we cannot admit our conscious feelings, we cannot control the behavior that follows from them. Irrational guilt limits our control over our own lives because it fosters denial.

CONSEQUENCES

Ralph was a gay man who had struggled with his homosexuality. His background was a pious Nazarene family that spent a lot of time in church. Getting married and having children was very important is this world. Homosexuality was deplored and denounced from the pulpit. The clear prohibition from Leviticus was cited over and over again. Ralph felt guilty about his feelings. He married a girl from high school. The marriage was a sexual disaster. It ended after six years with much bitterness and with Ralph feeling himself very much a sinner and a failure. After two years, Ralph found a male lover. They set up house together. Ralph found a job as a science teacher in an experimental private school. His new friend was a loving and caring companion. The relationship had every reason to succeed. But Ralph was tortured by guilt. The voice of Leviticus spoke to him every time he could attend to his private thoughts. When he felt frustrated by guilt he lashed out against his lover. His lover left him.

Ralph was the victim of "authoritarian thinking." A rule is a rule is a rule, especially if that rule has been endorsed by some prestigious authority, especially if it has been endorsed by someone who says he has spoken to God. *Authoritarians* never see rules as convenient summaries of human experience, which must always be tested by human experience. They see them as "beyond the human" proclamations, coming from some non-human source and indifferent to human consequences. Rules are absolute and have no exceptions. There are no extenuating circumstances. There are no evaluations. There are no revisions. At the most, there are interpretations.

The opposite of *authoritarians* are *consequentialists*. Consequentialists recognize the value of rules as useful guidelines from past human experience. But they do not regard them as absolute. Human experience spawned them. Human experience has the right to change them. There was nothing about Ralph's life that was harmful to society. An overpopulated world did not need more children. He was a useful and productive worker. He was a loving and caring friend. The one immoral thing he had done was to punish his lover for the sake of some inappropriate rule and the irrational guilt that it spawned. Ralph was not on trial. The rule was. And it failed.

Rational guilt is always testing rules. It is always paying attention to the consequences. If rules have been turned into public law by democratic choice, it will obey them even if it thinks that they are invalid. But it will work hard to change them. If public laws have outrageously bad consequences, if they prevent people from being useful and productive citizens by inhibiting their freedom and opportunities, then rational guilt will bravely resist them through civil disobedience.

Rational guilt never invokes some "higher law" that cancels out the "lower law." It is not interested in finding some more prestigious absolute rule to overrule the legislature. It does not appeal to God to veto the government. To do so is simply to compound the problem. The problem is absolute rules. It is one thing to work for the civil liberties of blacks in the name of some overriding divine love as Martin Luther King, Jr. did. It is another thing to practice civil disobedience in the name of what is good for society, of what will strengthen the social contract. Whites do not have to love blacks in order to be fair. And what is fair can only be tested by human experience. Even love is not always appropriate in the struggle for freedom. Sometimes anger is more appropriate.

Consequentialists are unpretentious. They never hide behind old and famous laws. They never pretend to be the voice of God. They just appeal to the facts and let them speak for themselves.

USEFULNESS

Grant was always talking about his freedom, about his freedom to do whatever he wanted to do with his life. Having been raised in an affluent, permissive family of the '70's he resisted all intrusion on his autonomy. When he left Michigan State University in his third year and moved to Colorado to ski full time, he defended his action by making his usual pitch for self-determination. When even his permissive parents, guilt-ridden at the thought of making any demand on their son, spoke out against his choice, he retaliated by throwing their old autonomy talk back in their faces. "Who are you to control my life?" They suggested that he was wasting his talents and failing in his social obligation to be a useful citizen. He was an extraordinary designer who had always expressed the hope of becoming an architect. Grant resisted their evaluation by claiming that only he knew what was best for him. The thought of being a social parasite was unimportant to him. He had no obligation to be useful to others. His only obligation was to his own freedom and to the voice of God within him.

For Grant there were only two criteria for right behavior, his own individuality and freedom, and the little internal voice of his personal conscience, which amounted to pretty much the same thing. Grant and God were always in agreement, now that God had been reduced to a message inside Grant. The thought that God had now become Grant's convenient puppet never occurred to Grant. Social usefulness in the name of some social contract was simply a "guilt trip" imposed by "uptight pseudo-liberals."

Rational guilt repudiates this narcissism. It finds it perfectly appropriate to discuss the social consequences of an individual's personal life style. It finds it perfectly appropriate to make people feel guilty for wasting their talents and living as social parasites. It finds it morally "OK" to point out that personal happiness often comes from social usefulness, from serving the needs of other people and receiving their approval for a job well done. We are social beings. Evolution has brought together our pleasure and our utility.

The current environmental movement, which has captured the allegiance of so many young people around the world, is an example of the need for responsible living. We either clean together or we die together. But environmentalism is not simply a personal love affair with nature, a dramatic protest against machine culture. It is a serious commitment to using whatever means are available to making this world safe for humanity. It means using new technology to clean up the effects of old technology. It means controlling our consumerism. It means the restriction of our personal freedom to live any way we want.

Rational guilt does not imagine that personal freedom and social responsibility are always compatible. We have an obligation to be more than we may want to be. We have an obligation to be useful citizens. We have an obligation to direct our talents to strengthening the social contract. We may discover, along the way, that helping others may be more pleasurable than self-indulgence.

TRANSCENDENCE

Ethical transcendence is different from spiritual transcendence. Ethical transcendence is the awareness of our powerful connection to other human beings. It is the sense that we and other people are part of some greater whole that evolution has blindly "arranged" to guarantee human survival. Human genes are not *"interested"* in individuals. They are *"interested"* in immortality. They *"use"* individuals as transmitters of their genetic agenda. Human individuals are shelters for their genetic masters. Communities are genetic pools and opportunities for new and creative mixing. Along the way they nurture individuals and allow them to nurture each other.

Ethical transcendence takes place in the hustle and bustle of the struggle for human survival and happiness. Nervous people work together to confront nerve-shattering problems. They stumble along the way. They hurt each other. They fight each other. They make up. Nothing is peaceful for very long. Even primitive man, so dependent on the help of a few others against the overwhelming dangers of nature, found existence often mean, brutish and short. But the connection with others was irresistible and indispensable.

Spiritual transcendence is quite different. It prefers peace and quiet, harmony and relaxation, escape and love. It cannot really find these things in the real world of daily existence. It needs to withdraw from the noisy world of facts. It needs to search for another world beyond this one, or within this one, of which the facts are only a suggestion. Some spiritual searchers, in their quest for the supernatural, withdraw from society and pursue their search by spending their time with less provocative parts of nature than people, or through the contemplation of the heavens, or through intense introspection. They seek a non-ethical posture called permanent relaxation. *Serenity* is the preferred word of the "spiritualists." What is *is*. No event makes them angry.

Rational guilt is not part of spiritual transcendence. It is too mundane, too loaded with hesitant judgment, too quick with anger, too oppressive with social obligations. It has trouble with personal agendas as big as the universe. Its focus is the human struggle on a small planet. In its agenda, finding the "heart of the universe" is less important than removing pollution from the rivers. It is impatient with pretentious diversions. It does not want to run away from problems simply because they give us a headache.

Ethical transcendence does not give you peace of mind. It gives you continuous tension, especially the tension between the whole and the part, between the individual and the community. Evolution produced a conflict. On the one hand there evolved guilt and a sense of collective identity. On the other hand, there evolved the human brain and the possibility of self-awareness. Individuals emerged with their own agendas and with the power of their critical judgment. Guilt drew them to the community. Self-awareness drew them to self-assertion and to the desire for personal freedom. The two evolutionary changes were on a collision course with each other. Guilt saw no reason why individuals should not subordinate themselves to collective solidarity. Self-awareness saw no reason why individuals should not assert themselves and should not refuse to be the masochistic fodder for some larger agenda.

Human nature does not possess some peaceful internal harmony. It is the setting for a war, the war of guilt against the selfishness of self-awareness. Ethics competes against self-preservation. The human mind is now too aware of its own separateness and individuality to blindly follow the dictates of group togetherness. It is no longer as comfortable as it once was with ethical transcendence. Once affluence loosened the bonds of mutual dependence and urban culture fostered the mobile individual, the philosophy of selfishness was inevitable.

Ayn Rand and her Objectivist ideology were a bold attempt to resolve this tension between the individual and the community, between freedom and guilt. Rand opted for the individual and freedom. She despised the community and guilt. Stealing ethics from guilt, she married it to freedom. Morality was turned upside down. Self-awareness and selfishness became virtues. Group identity and altruism became sins. Conventional words took on unconventional meanings. It was as though God had turned into the Devil.

But Rand's response to the internal war of the human soul was peevish and unrealistic. Ethics may coincide with self-interest some of the time. But it does not coincide with self-interest all of the time. There are times when group survival demands self-sacrifice. Conventional wisdom knows that the part sometimes gives itself up for the sake of the whole.

It does no good to elevate selfishness to a supreme value. Too much of human happiness is tied to guilt and ethical behavior. Group solidarity and the approval of comrades are intense pleasures for most human beings. Finding immortality in group survival is a common experience. We are programmed to do the work of guilt and be happy, much more so then to do the work of selfishness and be happy. If happiness is a rational goal in life, it cannot be achieved through self-absorption.

Rational guilt is the balancing act between selfishness and masochism. It uses enough guilt to keep society pasted together. But it champions enough freedom to allow for pleasurable self-assertion. The mix is never totally satisfactory. Discovering the fine line of balance is never easy. The tension rarely goes away. It defines the human condition.

14

MAKING MYSELF STRONG
Step 9

"WHERE AM I GOING TO FIND THE
strength to deal with my life?" Someone asked me that question
just before I sat down to write this chapter. It was an echo of a thousand identical questions that people have addressed to me over the
years. The questioner, of course, did not really expect me to answer.
Her question was rhetorical, an expression of her distress.

Her distress is real. She is a young mother of two infant
children who has just discovered that she has breast cancer. Her life has
been turned upside down. She is paralyzed by fear and anger. She is
bewildered. She does not have the will to make decisions. She feels
weak and inadequate. She feels sorry for herself and wants to cry.

Looking for strength is a normal human quest. Most people feel that they do not have the power or the will to cope with all that life deals out to them. There are too many problems to handle. There are too many decisions to make. It would be so nice to have a big storehouse of strength that we could draw from to replenish our meager supply.

The success of religion is a testimony to this wish. Gods are interesting and important because they are powerful, because they have strength to give. A good god without power has no significance. He has nothing to offer. Prayer and worship have been the avenues to divine power. In almost all cultures when people feel week and needy they pray. They ask for the gift of strength and power. They hope that the gods will infuse their bodies with new vigor and courage. They are eager in their felt helplessness for some kind of supernatural support.

But once you dismiss the *grand illusion* this power is no longer available. Like a meaningful universe it recedes into fantasy. The only power we can safely rely on is our own power and the power of other people. If we cannot find it within ourselves, we most likely will never find it. But how do we manufacture what we feel we do not have?

The first step is to understand the meaning of strength. For some people strength is physical. It is the energy to run, to jump, to work, to fight. The more energy the more strength; the more muscles the more power. Certainly, without physical strength, life becomes difficult if not impossible. Frail and sick people know how hard it is to get through the day without the energy that even simple tasks require.

But strength is more than physical. It is also mental. We all know many people of great physical power and energy who are mentally, very weak. And we also know many people of little physical power and energy who are mentally very strong. Even sick people may compensate for their physical frailty with mental strength.

Mental strength is the strength of our will. It is the strength of the decision making power of our brain. The heart and kidneys may be weak and failing. But, if the brain is strong, if the mind is focused with determination on important tasks, it may prevail.

Avery is a tall "strong" man. He is very muscular and very athletic. When you first meet him you think of power. His handshake is firm and tight, with a just so slight edge of intimidation. His posture is straight and commanding. His voice is deep and booming. When he walks down the street even muggers run away. But Avery is a mental *nebbish*. His problem is that he cannot make a decision. He suffers from what Walter Kaufmann, the Princeton philosopher, called "decidophobia." Avery is still in Ann Arbor after ten years of undergraduate agony. His difficulty is not academic competence. If he can bring himself to complete a course, his grade is more than satisfactory. But, he has difficulty deciding what term papers to write. There are so many topics to pick from. It is so hard to know which one is the right one for him. It is easier to wait until he is sure. "Incompletes" are better than failures. He has difficulty choosing a major. He likes both political science and psychology. He feels that he would be a good lawyer. He also feels that he would be a good psychologist. He has interviewed dozens of lawyers and psychologists. Every time he is with one or the other he is convinced that their profession is the one for him. He wants to make a choice. But he knows that you have to be careful. A wrong choice would be very embarrassing and expensive. Postponing the decision is certainly the wisest thing to do. Maybe tomorrow some new piece of evidence will make the difference for him. Avery has difficulty choosing a lover and wife. Women are very attracted to him. His handsome face and body are instant turn-ons. But, he is never sure that he has chosen the right one. He always asks his friends about how they feel about his current lover. He would love to make a commitment. He says that all the time. But, before he has a chance to postpone his decision one more time, his lover leaves in frustration. He has to start again from scratch. The one area of his life where he is decisive is food. He always orders hamburgers. It feels wonderful to be committed to eating one food, and one food alone. It relieves a person of the burden of choosing.

Avery's problem is that the muscles of his will have nothing to do with the muscles of his body. They are underdeveloped. He is a weak mind in a strong body—far worse than a strong mind in a weak body. He is ripe for plucking by some kind of authoritarian cult. They will make decisions for him. They will take responsibility for his life.

Being mentally weak can drive you crazy. A crazy world gives you no guarantees of success and happiness. It offers you no assurance that hard work will result in personal victory. There is this terrible uncertainty. There is this terrible risk. In time, you become just as crazy as the world you live in. Chaos and fear take over. The freedom to choose becomes a terrifying burden. You lose control of your life.

Mental strength is essential to sanity. It is the energy of order that fights the chaos and craziness of the world. An ambiguous universe does not need our invitation. It needs resistance. It needs the force of our will. The certainty of our commitment meets the uncertainty of its message.

The human will has its roots in our consciousness and self-awareness. It emerged with our power to reason. It gives us the power to choose. It is comparatively new. Like reason, it is fighting older and deeper powers in our unconscious mind. When it is paralyzed by ambivalence and indecision, our behavior still continues, guided by unconscious emotional focus we neither know nor understand.

Many people today believe that these unconscious powers are good and benevolent. We need to make contact with them. We need to trust them. We need to yield to them. So much of the new mysticism deplores ego and will. If only we give ourselves up to our deep intuitions, all will be well. But all is not well when that happens. The unconscious mind is as torn by indecision as the conscious mind. Avery's annoying ambivalence is not only a response to an uncertain world. It is also a reflection of his confused unconscious unable to energize his paralyzed will, unable to provide clear direction.

In the end, there is no substitute for will. If it is strong our life has a chance for sanity and purpose. If it is weak, then we become crazy wanderers in a crazy universe, victims of an equally crazy unconscious. Fear, anger, love and hate have been competing so long for our energies in the deepest recesses of our minds, that to put them in charge of our lives without a strong leader is to invite chaos.

What do we have to do to make our will stronger than it is? Training involves at least five affirmations.

MY OPINION IS OBVIOUSLY MY OPINION

Strong people prefer open and direct communication. While, like most people, they have their vulnerable areas, they do not resist the strong opinions of others. Disagreement and debate are not signs of failure. They are the path to discovering the truth.

Over the past twenty years conversation in America has taken a depressing turn. In the new age of egalitarian politics and subjective truth, people are reluctant to be too pushy about what they believe. Parents and teachers are more cautious. They do not want to drive their children and students away. They do not want to appear authoritarian or dogmatic. They do not want to suggest that there may be some single objective truth.

Men and women today frequently prepare their remarks by saying, "well, in my opinion" or "well, it's only my opinion," as though it was news that their opinion is their opinion—or as though having an opinion was an intrusive frivolous action barely worthy of acknowledgement. We now live in the age when telling other people that they are wrong is a violation of democratic ethics. Your opinion is your opinion. And my opinion is my opinion. Communication is only a "sharing." It is never a real discussion. A real discussion is an attempt to arrive at some objective truth. "Sharing" is nothing more than that—a sharing of two subjective truths within the framework of a timid courtesy. "Sharing" is as vacuous as an indecisive will. In fact, it is one of the reasons why so many people can never make up their minds. If all truth is subjective, if your opinion is just as good as my opinion, then there is no reliable truth I can depend on to make any decision. Knowledge becomes an amorphous mush. And the will follows.

Weak people have no commitment to objective truth. They just want to be nice. They listen and share—and never confront. Strong people have a commitment to discerning reality. They want to discuss the evidence. They want to find out what is really going on. They already know that their opinion is their opinion. They have no reason to state the obvious.

DEALING WITH THE WORLD AS IT IS

Realistic people do not fight reality. They may prefer it to be different, but they are willing to work with what they have. If they want to change it or improve it, they have to start with where the world is, not where their expectations are.

Lois had trouble with the men she dated. She was a forty year old divorcee with two children and eager for a loving and understanding husband. The men she met at Parents without Partners did not exactly conform to the image of the handsome prince she had treasured for many years. She said to herself that she would have to compromise but the reality was far worse than she ever imagined. Some were whiny complainers who never stopped talking about their personal agonies for an entire evening. Others were "flakes" who told her that she was the most fabulous woman they had ever met and then had never bothered to call. Still others were "pigs," quickly uttering seductive and obscene invitations and pawing her on the first date. Lois was traumatized. She could not stop talking about how bad the dating scene was. She contemplated celibacy. Meanwhile, her friend Edna, who was less intolerant than she was and more realistic, persisted in her search. She found Fred, a loving and nurturing man—who had called Lois first, only to be visited by a curt refusal. Lois was too impatient with reality. She missed her opportunity.

We cannot punish reality by getting angry at it. The dating scene is often nasty and brutal. But it is no more nasty and brutal than the work scene—or even the family scene. Gross self-absorbed people abound everywhere. Even we, if there was no fear of punishment, might behave in a similar way. Privacy and anonymity frequently turn saints into devils. Being realistic about percentages is essential to sanity and success.

What we consider to be a success many others deem to be a failure. If I chair a committee and twenty percent of my committee works hard, I feel very good about my achievement. My unrealistic friend accomplishes the same *feat* and always imagines that she has failed. She wants the world to be different from what it is and judges herself by a standard appropriate to a fantasy universe. Strong people do not doctor the figures so that they always appear to be winners. But they refuse to be perpetual losers, just because reality is different from what they expected. Having high standards is different from having high expectations. The first makes you more persistent. The second makes you surrender too soon.

POSTPONING DECISIONS HAS ITS LIMITS

Life does not give us the luxury of waiting forever. If we do not make decisions at the right time, the opportunity vanishes and we are left with useless speculation. Jobs demand decisions before we know everything about them. Friendships demand commitments before we are absolutely sure that they will work. Aging time-clocks push us to the wall before we know for sure that we will love having children. Most decisions have an *iffy* quality to them. They need to be made before we enjoy complete certainty. And waiting for complete certainty is like waiting for forever.

Weak people always complain about time limitations. They often ignore them. They plead helplessness. "After all, you can't expect me to make a decision if I don't have all the facts." They fail to realize that avoiding a decision is really making a decision—making a decision to do nothing.

> Linda wanted to enter the literary contest. She loved her short story. But it was not completely what she wanted. There were two or three flawed paragraphs. She brought the manuscript to her creative writing teacher. He read the story. He loved it. He told her that she ought to stop struggling with the paragraphs and submit the document before the deadline the next day. The flaws were minor but Linda was a perfectionist. Nothing was ever as good as she wanted it to be. She missed the deadline. And that became the story of her literary career.

Perfectionists, like indecisive fact-finders, are always waiting for what never arrives. They always miss the deadlines of life. They are like Robert who never finished his doctoral dissertation because it was less than sensational. The allotted time passed. He could not bear mediocrity. Failure was preferable to imperfection.

For perfectionists postponing decisions may be convenient. They never have to face the consequences of risky decisions. They never have to court failure. They are safe losers who can always claim that they would be winners if only they had the time to do everything that needed to be done—or to find out what needed to be discovered.

Strong people can live with risk and imperfection. They believe that failure is worse. They believe that too much caution kills the value of life. They do not welcome deadlines. But they respect them. Life is too short to be compulsively careful. It will not wait for us.

"Wise men weigh the advantages of any course of action

against its drawbacks and move not an inch until they can see what the result of their action will be. But, while they are deep in thought, the men with self-confidence come and see and "conquer." So said Ahad Haam, a twentieth century Jewish philosopher. (*Ahad Haam*, by Leon Simon)

TAKING PAIN WITH THE PLEASURE

Most pain is useless suffering. But some pain is useful. It is a prelude to pleasure. Like labor pains before the baby, like tedious study before the graduation, like hard work before the promotion—useful pain is the price reality expects for happiness. As Freud pointed out, our pleasure principle needs the discipline of our reality principle. Weak people are often impulsive people. They love to praise spontaneity. They love to make fun of "square" people who worry about the consequences. They prefer "now" to "later." They are impatient with waiting. In fact, they cannot bear it.

> Fred loved audiences. He thrived on their attention and applause. In high school he was the lead in the senior play. There was something wonderful about acting. The people were right there in front of you, giving you the pleasure of their approval. He always had trouble studying. Study was such a lonely profession. Hours and hours of tedious labor were wasted in a play without an audience. Fred paced himself. He would study for two hours. And then he would go out with the boys for pizza or coffee. He added a few too many pounds from the pizza. But the daily audience provided him with relief. And in high school he could get by with two hours of study a day because he was smart and the

demands were small. When he arrived at the university things changed. The demands were so much greater he had little time for friends. He became depressed from the isolation of study. He found a friend to study with. But an audience of one was not enough to turn him on. He loved political science. He wanted to go to law school. The drama of the court room excited him. But it seemed so far away. He joined a fraternity. Planning fraternity parties was his *cup of tea*. They boys adored him. He stopped studying. He flunked out of school. Fred became a salesman. He made good money in men's clothing. He was jealous of his achieving friends, especially those who graduated from law school. He pretended not to care. He called himself a "now" person. He always told jokes because he wanted people to laugh. Sometimes he could not stop telling jokes. He became pathetic, too desperate for attention. He thought of going back to school and completing his studies. But the discipline of study frightened him. He justified his failure by saying that the fates made him the way he was. There was nothing he could do about it.

Strong people do not assume that strength comes only from the fates. Some strength comes from training. Postponing pleasure is not easy. The infant in us craves immediate gratification. Strong people reward themselves with the images of future gratification. While they endure the tedious toil of preparing for success they imagine what the future will bring and caress themselves with positive expectations. They also scare themselves with images of failure. They imagine what not completing the work will mean. Pleasures of the imagination can sometimes be as real as the pleasures of the senses. Focused anticipation can be a wonderful disciplinarian.

Before I completed my undergraduate degree at the University of Michigan I had to write three very long term papers—two in philosophy and one in political science. I had procrastinated to the last term and amused myself with intercollegiate debating. Only one week remained before the due date of the papers. I had done nothing. As the reality of my situation sank into my conscious, I panicked. How would I ever be able to do what I needed to do in such a short time.

But I had to do it. I had no real choice. I sat down, divided up my time among the three papers, so much time for research, so much time for outlining, so much time for writing. The act of taking control and planning eased my panic. And, as I sat down to begin my discipline, I let my mind wander from pleasant anticipation to scary scenarios. I saw myself rescuing my degree from the very hand of the university president. I saw my mother crying, crushed by the news that I had failed to finish my course of study in time. The images gave me motivation. Every so often I would stop and linger on them, changing details of the final scene as I went along. My internal reward and punishment proved effective—three term papers in one week. I discovered that I was stronger than I imagined.

PREFERRING RESPECT TO APPROVAL

There are two kinds of approval. There is the approval which parents give to children. It is turned on by vulnerability, sweetness and obedience. It is reinforced by reverence, admiration and loving deference. By its very nature it is patronizing. There is also the approval which peers give to peers. It is turned on by power and strength. It is reinforced by courage and self-reliance. By its very nature it is a combination of fear and attraction. We call it respect.

Weak people never grow out of their infant strategies. For

them desirable approval is patronizing approval. Neither respect nor admiration is what they want. What they want is that cuddly approval that children thrive on. But they have to pay the price for it. They always have to conform. They always have to obey. They must never confront nor challenge. When we are patronized we recognize that our status is inferior. The appeal of patronizing approval is that it comes from a superior and confers legitimacy on what we do. There is both a graciousness and a threat to the act of its bestowal. If we do what we are told to do we will be lovingly protected. But, if we defy our superiors and refuse to conform to their demands, they will beat us with the whip of dismissal. Weak people toe the line because there is no other way to get approval.

Strong people repudiate their infant strategies. They do not want to be patronized. They want to be respected and admired. They know that the strategy of respect is quite different from that of reverent obedience. They know that the strategy of respect is not the same as worship and humility. The approval they desire is the approval that comes from equals. And that approval often begins with disapproval.

Michael was a loving and obedient son. His mother was an elegant aloof woman who was stingy with compliments. From childhood on Michael tried to please his mother. But she was not easily pleased. The more she refused him approval the harder he tried. From time to time she would relent and embrace him with her quietly stated, "That was wonderful Michael." When she deigned to say those words, Michael became ecstatic. Had some billionaire given him all his fortune he could not have been happier. But most of the time she was moody and indifferent, unimpressed by anything he did. Of course, her aloofness made her approval his obsession. Three years ago Michael, who was a senior in the business school, met an exciting woman in his economics class. She was elegant but warm and very intelligent. They fell in love. They decided to live together. They decided to get married. But there was a problem. Although neither was very religious, Michael was Jewish and April, his fiancee, was Catholic. They decided to have both their cultural backgrounds represented in their wedding celebration. After much difficulty, they found both a priest and a rabbi who would co-officiate. The rabbi was me. When April told her widowed mother about the arrangements she was supportive. She had come to love Michael and to welcome him into her home as her very own son. But when Michael told his mother about their plans, she became hostile. Never losing her *cool*, she expressed her strong disapproval. While she liked April and thought that she was good for Michael, she would not attend a wedding for her son where a priest was present and officiated. When Michael protested that she had never been religious and that her decision was hypocritical, she devastated Michael by saying, "I am very disappointed in you Michael." Michael could not continue the conversation. He could not endure his mother's disapproval. He walked out of his mother's house and began to cry from frustration. That evening he had an argument with April. He told her that he was uncomfortable with having a priest at the wedding. She accused him of being a "mamma's boy," unable to think for himself. She left him. He came to see me.

I reminded Michael that getting married meant that your spouse was now the most important person in your life next to yourself, more important than your mother and your father. If he did not believe that, he should not be getting married. I also reminded him that he needed a new relationship with his mother. He needed more than her approval. He needed her respect. To get that he would have to stand up to her. He would have to confront her with the decision that April and he had jointly reached—and that he would have to risk her disapproval. He winced when he heard the word "disapproval." But he continued to listen and nodded his agreement.

Two days later Michael and April went to see Michael's mother. She was very pleasant and conciliatory. She imagined that they had arrived to announce their capitulation. But, Michael surprised her. He told her that the decision they had made would not be changed. It was fair and respectful to both cultures. It was something they felt very comfortable with. They hoped that she understood that their wedding was their wedding—and, although there was disagreement, she was very important to them. Michael told his mother that he loved her very much. When Michael finished, his mother launched into a tirade. She was insulted. She would never attend. She was, for the first time in her life, absolutely devastated. Although shaking, Michael held his ground. He told his mother that, as she was disappointed in him, he was equally disappointed in her. When April and he left his mother's house, April noticed a new self-confidence in Michael. He had done something he had never done before. He had confronted his mother as an equal, and that confrontation had altered his self-image. He was no longer the compliant son. He was no longer willing to be patronized. He was demanding respect. And that is what he ultimately got. His mother continued to threaten her boycott.

But she ultimately made her appearance at the ceremony, hesitant but gracious. Her communication with Michael changed. She had experienced his strength and integrity. Things would never be the same. She now offered him her respect. In time, she would add admiration.

Strong people want respect, not patronizing approval. They know that sometimes the right kind of approval starts with the risk of disapproval. When they receive respect from the people they respect, they experience the beginning of self-esteem.

MY POWER IS MY POWER

A very successful minister in my home town was an alcoholic. At one point in his life, he reached rock-bottom. He found Alcoholics Anonymous. He followed the Twelve Steps. He rescued himself. Along the way he also found the "Higher Power" that is an essential ingredient of the program. The alcoholic must surrender his will to that Higher Power and allow it to guide him to recovery. Only if he feels that some power external to him is leading the way, will he be able to follow. The spiritual experience of a guiding providence is an important part of the transformation.

When the minister recovered he came to believe that what had worked for him would work for everybody, even non-alcoholics. He established his own church, preached an open liberal non-dogmatic religion—very much like Alcoholics Anonymous—and made the Higher Power the center of his spiritual message. Coping with the problems of life could only be joyous and successful if each person found his Higher Power, underwent this spiritual experience. God was no supervisor of heaven or hell. He was a celestial friend who was there to give you that spiritual extra to push you over the top.

Since the minister was a charismatic and extraordinary preacher, thousands flocked to hear him. He shared with them his story of his climb from the depths to recovery. He told them they too could experience the same redemption, no matter what the problem. Many of the people who came and stayed were recovering alcoholics. But most of the people were people with conventional problems. In time his devotees became so enthusiastic they began to spread the word. There was a slight edge of self-righteousness to their message. Unless you found a Higher Power just as they did, your life would never be really meaningful.

Now I watched the development of this congregation with admiration. Many people were deeply moved by the minister's message. Many people claimed that he had helped them to change their lives for the better. The format was an open liberal spirituality. But there was an annoying edge to all this joy and self-congratulations. While I recognized that the message helped many people I also recognized the *grand illusion*. From the realistic perspective the power that had rescued them was their own power. But if they acknowledged that it was their own power the magic would be gone. Only by believing that a benevolent force other then their own was guiding their recovery could they benefit from the discipline. In the end their so-called strength rested on their weakness. The Higher Power was the "crutch" of their recovery. And it was not a temporary "crutch." It was a permanent one.

All of this development would have been sustainable if they had kept their enthusiasm to themselves. But their insistence on presenting weakness as strength continued to annoy me. I began to reflect on my annoyance. Why was I so bothered by the message? Was it because weak people who needed a "crutch" did not see their "crutch" and were now pretentiously lecturing strong people on how to be strong? Or was it that turning everybody into a recovering alcoholic seemed a bit pushy, a not so subtle way of classifying everybody as needy or sick? Or was it that much larger issue of owning up to your own power, of giving yourself credit for what you were doing, of giving up the low esteem of the child who attributes all his power to his parents.

I liked and admired the minister. But, as a realist, I believe that he deserved more credit than he gave himself or gave to others. The Higher Power that "rescued" him must have been the same power that gave him his genetic vulnerability to alcohol, that allowed him to sink to the depths, that abandoned him before it "saved" him. It is amazing to me how needy people can hide from what they do not want to see. When in a moment of desperation, the minister sought help from a group of caring men and women in AA, they nurtured him. But he could not give them credit for what they did. He responded to their nurturing by helping himself. But he could not give himself credit for what he did.

One of the signs of personal strength is that we take the blame for what we do wrong. The other sign is that we take credit for what we do right. We do not alienate our power by assigning it to someone outside ourself. Realists have enough opportunities to acknowledge their limitations. But they also take time to recognize their power.

Weak people cannot acknowledge their own power. They do not believe that they have any. In the end, if they find that they have power, it cannot be their own power. It must come from somewhere else. Strong people are comfortable recognizing their own power. They do not exaggerate. Nor do they minimize. Nor do they call their power a "Higher Power." It is their power.

Our society is now filled with many missionaries of the weak. Missionaries of the weak always diminish strong people by "taking away" their strength. Missionaries of the strong enhance weak people by encouraging them to face up to their own power. Realists are missionaries of the strong.

15

SEARCH FOR BEAUTY
Step 10

W HEN I FIRST SAW JOHN'S GAR-
den in Florida, I was almost transfixed. All I could say was, "how beautiful." The garden was planted along a winding path leading from the
back of his home to his pool. It was an open ordinary space that was
not easy to transform. But the flow of the colors and forms had created this radiant snake that lay as an adornment on the landscape. As
you walked down the pathway your eye was caught up in all the vari-
ety. There were begonias and hydrangea. There were flowers that
had no name for me but which embraced me with their loveliness.
There were heavy lush plants and fragile paper-thin petals. There was
even a surprising little enclave of cactus, gracing each other in a

kind of Zen simplicity. The garden was overwhelming and restful at the same time.

John told me that tending the garden was a unique experience for him. When he worked on it, all the cares of the outer world vanished and he felt a deep and abiding connection with the earth. He liked working with his hands. He liked touching and feeling the earth. His grandfather had been a farmer and he had pleasant memories of helping him out in the fields. His garden was his refuge, a quiet place where he could separate himself from the noise of outer distractions and exist in peace and harmony with the world. There were times, he said, that he felt so close to his flowers that they were almost like his very own children.

I listened to John carefully. I did not doubt that the garden was beautiful. That was obvious. I did not doubt that his work was deeply satisfying or that the garden was more quiet and more peaceful than the rest of the urban world. But I did not see the garden as some kind of easy harmony between John and nature. The garden was hard work. Like his grandfather's farm, the garden was a human creation, a tribute to human ingenuity. Keeping the garden beautiful was a continuous battle against the "enemies" of nature. Weeds had to be pulled up. Bugs had to be exterminated. Water had to be provided when the rains did not come. Agriculture, even in the form of backyard gardening, was no different from the labor of making a stone ax or designing a skyscraper. It was only restful because it was different. Farmers, after a hard day's work, love to go into town for distraction and relaxation.

After all, digging and planting in the soil is comparatively new for the human race. For most of human evolution our ancestors were hunters. Stalking and killing animals is our primitive inheritance. Farming began barely ten thousand years ago, a mere drop in the bucket of time from the perspective of human development. And once launched, agriculture transformed the landscape of nature. It cut down trees; it drained swamps; it cultivated land, it cut new rivers of water; it built villages. The countryside we love is the tailored countryside of the farmer. If the farmer is not careful it will turn back into weeds and brush and impenetrable swamps. Agriculture—and gardening—are no less "artificial" than building roads or sewers. Even the tools that gardeners use are the manufactured objects of urban civilization. Urban gardens can be beautiful. But they are no more "natural" than the plumbing in the house to which they are attached. Even some of the giant flowers in my friend's garden are the children of laboratories and genetic engineering.

When I see a beautiful garden I try to imagine what it would be like without human intervention. I see waist high clusters of weeds and ordinary plants. I see pesty bugs and hungry intruders. While I understand the spontaneous beauty we often discover in the wilderness and the jungle, I also understand that nature, left to its own devices, is as capable of producing ugliness as it is of producing beauty. Experiencing nature in the garden has nothing to do with experiencing nature in the raw.

Nature has to be tailored to fit human need. The human agenda and the flower-in-the-garden's agenda are not one and the same. The flower is our slave, to be used for whatever visual purposes we deem necessary. It is neither our brother nor our sister. It is certainly not our child. If it fails to fit into our scheme, it will be pulled up and discarded, just like the weeds. Our relationship is nurturing without commitment, a too fragile relationship for harmonious togetherness.

Nature mystics find beauty in everything that nature does.

Nature worship is part of the *grand illusion*. The alternative is to love beauty wherever it appears and wherever it is created.

Beauty is not trivial. Without beauty life would be intolerable. Beauty softens the harshness of a world without meaning. We cannot transform the moral appearance of the world. But we can stand in wonder of garden flowers, Mozart symphonies, Taj Mahals, and towering mountains. Some of the beauty we admire has arisen spontaneously from the evolution of the universe. Some of it has come from human invention.

But what is beauty? Why do we call some things beautiful and other things ugly? How do we make a distinction between the beautiful and the ordinary.

It is not easy to talk about beauty these days. In an egalitarian world it seems undemocratic to designate some people and some things beautiful and other people and other things ordinary. There is an elitist edge to aesthetics. Some people may end up with their feelings hurt. Some people may end up on the wrong side of the dividing line. Either you say that everything is beautiful—or you drop the word altogether.

But everything is not beautiful. There is the ordinary and the ugly in the world. Only someone into massive denial or into privileged premises would come up with the aesthetic equivalent of a moral Polyanna. If everything is beautiful then nothing is beautiful. *Beauty* only has meaning if there is something to contrast it with. People may not agree on what is beautiful or ugly—just as they do not agree on what is right and wrong—but they do agree that there is a difference.

The best way to discover what beauty is, is to look at the vast array of things which people of all cultures have called beautiful. Light and fire, vistas and open space, symmetry and order, health and fertility—are universal candidates for universal approval. What do these dissimilar phenomena have in common? What they have in common is their relationship to the satisfaction of basic human needs.

Without light there would be no life. Without fire, human culture and civilization would never have emerged. Without vistas our sharpest sense, seeing and vision, would be useless. Without order, we would never establish control over our environment. Without health we would be helplessly vulnerable. Without fertility we would have no future.

Things are beautiful in so far as they dramatize what we as humans need and want. If we were snakes and capable of the emotion of wonder, then we would have an entirely different list of wonders. Beauty is relative in the sense that it is related to human need. It is not some objective thing, out there, independent of human judgment. It is a subjective reality. But it is less than relative, as far as human beings are concerned, because we share most of our basic needs and desires. If we did not, then it would be impossible to create objects of beauty which other people would value.

Now beauty is not the same as usefulness. Beauty starts with useful things, experiences, and powers. But it goes beyond their usefulness. A simple table may be useful. It serves human need. But it may not be a beautiful table. What makes the table beautiful is its ability to dramatize the purpose for which it was created. It grabs your attention and makes you notice what you would otherwise take for granted. Beauty has some level of exaggeration. The table has more sides than it needs. The eyes of the face are bigger than survival requires. The light in the painting is more intense than the light of an ordinary day. What is useful is transformed into some dramatic focus of attention.

Beauty is, therefore, a symbol of life and of all that we

require for survival and happiness. By its very existence it conveys hope. That is why it inspires us. That is why it stimulates our wonder. Even when it is involved with the morbid themes of death and war, it suggests heroic defiance or inner strength. As human beings we thrive on symbols, especially the symbols that announce our commitment to life.

Of course, symbols vary from culture to culture. We build our symbols out of the materials and experiences of our environment. Mayan priests did not have snowy landscapes. Europeans did not have tigers. Egyptian artists did not have rain. We also build our symbols out of our beliefs, whether these beliefs be true or false. The vertical thrust of church interiors speaks of God. The serene smile of the Buddha statue points to mystical enlightenment. The Madonna and Child proclaim the maternal love of a loving universe. Realists can even see the beauty in symbols of the *grand illusion*, because, despite the illusion, they are symbols of hope.

Beauty may be attached to values which we used to applaud and which we now deplore. Warlike societies glorify the warrior. Military prowess and martial virtue have been beautiful in most historic cultures. The cult of youth and virility, so much a part of the Greek legacy, is part of this adoration. Modern fascism found special beauty in the energy and discipline of the soldier. Interestingly enough, modern bourgeois culture was never able to turn the businessman into a figure of beauty. At the most, the soldier was replaced by the sports hero. The cult of virility finds new ways to defend its social usefulness.

Beauty may also be attached to events which are terrifying in their human consequences. A forest fire burns, destroying life and property. One part of our mind imagines the charred trees and the howling of animals on fire. The other part is entranced by the soaring flames in the night's darkness. The burning destruction has its own beauty. The immediate impression of fire and light transcends the ghastly results.

But beauty, on the whole, remains a form of reassurance. It tells us that, in this world of undeserved pain and suffering, in this world of ugly fear and cowardice, there are counterforces of resistance. The cold encounters fire. Darkness encounters light. Death encounters life. The presence of beauty in the universe makes life worth living. The struggle for happiness is no futile exercise. While there are no guarantees of success, there is the possibility of victory.

Recognizing and cultivating beauty in our lives is a source of strength. Beauty nourishes our hopes in the same way that food nourishes our body. Realists seek out the aesthetic experience in the same way that mystics look for the spiritual. The "aesthetic fix" keeps them going.

But what exactly do realists do in their search for beauty?

ART

Most of the beauty in the world is tied to circumstance. We notice it and enjoy it. But we do not create it. Art is a human creation. It is the deliberate attempt to "manufacture" beauty. Anything that is really art aims for beauty. Bad art fails. Good art succeeds.

An artist friend recently told me that he resented the elitist imperialism of the past which tied art to some vague notion of beauty. For him artistic expression was the expression of the right brain as opposed to the communication of the left brain. Art was the intuitive emotional side of human communication as opposed to the rational side. I asked him whether every emotional intuitive utterance was art. Was screaming at my friend art? Was my enraged ramming of the car in front of me art? Was my faith in the ultimate victory of the Detroit Pistons art? After all, there was no form of human communication that did not have some element of emotion and intuition. The right and left brain worked in tandem. Whatever came out of our behavior was a mixture of reason and emotion. Even usually recognized great art involved some degree of rational planning and structure on the part of the artist. There was no pure emotion. There was no pure reason.

The problem of living in an egalitarian age is that we are afraid to render any objective judgment. All opinions are of equal value, because all people are of equal value. Truth is no longer a function of evidence. It is a function of whatever we want it to be. Art is no longer a function of beauty. It is whatever we declare it to be. We have moved from the dogmas of traditional faith to its polar opposite. A crazy world is rendered crazier by removing from it what might give life some shared meaning. A democratic chaos now replaces the old authoritarian posture.

The world of formal art has shifted its focus. Having lost the criterion of beauty, it now suffers the disease of "originality" and "creativity." The purpose of artistic expression is not to produce something beautiful. It is to invent something different. The more conventional and familiar my creation the worse. The more bizarre and exotic my creation the better. Art becomes tied to the gimmicks of originality. "I am innovative, therefore I am good" becomes the cry of the desperate search for reality. Dissonance may be novel. It may be an expression of the disharmonies of our society. But it is not beautiful. It offers no reassurance. Listening to it is like having to do homework. It always has to be explained.

Now dissonance and ugliness may be part of a great artistic work. Good art may feature suffering, death, pain, violence, failure and depression. Dostoyevsky and Kafka were hardly cheerleaders of joy. Aeschylus and Shakespeare were familiar with tragedy. But their setting was the solemn grandeur of the human struggle, the confrontation of the individual with the cruelty of unkind fates. The human resistance to this destiny, whether meek or defiant, has its own beauty, even though the ending is failure. Hope lies in the power of the human spirit, not in the happy resolution of the struggle. Great art allows us to experience despair. But it does not allow us to wallow in it.

Merely reliving pain, suffering and violence is no foundation of good art. Without the hint of human resistance the suffering becomes a morbid fascination devoid of beauty. The gratuitous violence of the contemporary cinema and television testifies to the emptiness of so much modern art. It is depressing. The story is unredeemable. Only the technology and the performance of the actors warrants admiration.

Human resistance does not mean the romantic nonsense of John Galt in *Atlas Shrugged*. But John Galt is preferable to mindless mayhem. Like promiscuous sex for those in search of love, it gives you a temporary high at the price of a lingering emptiness. Where beauty is absent—art fails. Art does not need to be Pollyannish to be hopeful. But it does have to indicate even some *smidgeon* of human grandeur and resistance.

The most successful art forms of contemporary culture are not recognized by artistic snobs. They are sports events. In the graceful *"dances"* of baseball, football, basketball and hockey—in the vital energy of tennis, golf, swimming and running—heroes of risk and defiance display the beauty of their skills. Each contest is a testimony to human ingenuity and talent. A fast-moving basketball game, with its miracle passes and its mind-boggling bursts and turns, is a much more exciting ballet than standing on your toes. The ancient Greeks saw the connection between beauty and athletics. So does the sports-loving "philistine" of the contemporary world, even though he may not be able to articulate his vision.

Artistic snobs deplore the indifference of the masses to their new experimental art. They imagine that art is confined to galleries and performance halls. They do not do justice to the hunger of the masses for the inspiration of beauty. They are unable to celebrate the joy of millions who fill massive stadiums to celebrate the defiant grace of sports heroes. Eager fans stomp and cheer for feats of glory which they themselves cannot perform but which suggest the possibility of the human potential. Even with too much beer and hot dogs these games of skill are much more inspiring than champagne at gallery openings in Soho.

Sports is the supreme art form of the modern world. Nothing else celebrates the beauty of the human form more triumphantly. Sporting events are not merely cathartic substitutes for war. They are celebrations of beauty and feed the human spirit with the hope of human resistance. Much more than religion they alleviate the craziness of a crazy world. That is why football games have better attendance than church services. The artistic rituals are much more exciting.

ENVIRONMENT

Finding beauty in the world around us is so important for alleviating the frustration of daily life. "Getting away" to lovely places restores our energies. We surround ourselves by beauty and rediscover our hope.

Most people imagine that "nature" is more beautiful than the artificial settings of modern cities. They see this dichotomy between

the fertile life-giving "outdoors" and the sterile oppressive polluted setting of the urban "indoors." They fancy the refreshing experience of
mountain streams, leafy forests and wilderness trails. They deplore the
stale experience of cement pathways in concrete canyons.

One of my friends has become a "nature freak." An early envi-
ronmentalist he only has nasty things to say about the therapeutic possibilities of cities. He thinks that they are ugly. No skyscraper, in his
mind, can compete with the beauty of a mountain. Skyscrapers are
artificial and, therefore, inferior. Mountains are natural and, therefore,
superior. Urban settings are nasty prisons. The outdoors is liberation.
I recently accepted an invitation to his wilderness paradise. I lasted for
only one day. Giant flies and mosquitoes drove me home. He admitted that they were annoying—but not as annoying as breathing auto
fumes. When he retired from work two years ago I imagined that he
would retire to his cabin up in northern Michigan. But he lingered in
suburban Detroit. When I confronted him with the seeming uncertainty of his choice, he admitted that he had trouble understanding
his own behavior.

I did not have as much trouble understanding his behavior. I
know many people who suffer from the same ambivalence—and
the same denial. Nature is beautiful. But not all of it. From pesky
mosquitoes to the volcanic ash of Mount Pinatubo, there are aspects
of nature that are less than friendly to people. And from indoor
plumbing to night life there are sides to city living that are very
attractive. Most people stay in city environments—not because they
hate them or because they cannot find work elsewhere—but because
urban settings are more exciting and stimulating than natural ones.

In reality the contrast between nature and the "artificial"
environment of the cities is phony. Whatever life does is natural.
When robins build nests, that is natural. When beavers create dams

that is natural. When spiders spin webs that is natural. When humans tend farms and build cities that is natural. The human brain is not unnatural. It is just as natural as the dog's tail. What the human brain can do is just as natural as what the snake's brain can do. Separating humans and human activity from nature is about as reasonable as separating the last act of a play from the play itself. When human activity is beneficial to humans and to other living beings it is natural. When human activity is harmful to humans and to other living beings it is also natural. Nature has many faces. Some are beautiful. Some are ugly.

Nature, in and of itself, is neither all beautiful nor all ugly. Sometimes it needs to be made more beautiful. That is what environmentalism is all about. The human brain has to figure out how to promote human survival and human happiness. Eliminating cities will not remove all pollution in a world of poisonous volcanic eruptions and swampy miasmas. Saving all living creatures will not be a loving act in a world of Lyme ticks and cancer viruses. Promoting organic food over man-made nutrition will not be helpful on a planet filled with lethal mushrooms and cane sugar. Loving nature is loving all that is beautiful in nature. Loving all that is beautiful in nature is promoting all that enhances human survival. Enhancing human survival is finding the proper balance between the wilderness and skyscrapers. Nature is a long spectrum of opportunity, ranging from concrete roads through tailored gardens cultivated fields and planned parks to "untouched" jungle. No one stop along the way is the right stop. Realistic people use all their opportunities. They know that the worship of nature "in the raw" is a silly fanaticism. They also know that nature has no single agenda. They are good-humored enough to realize that beauty is part of the human agenda. That is why we want to save "wise" owls more than slimy algae. At least we can identify with them.

The ethics of environmentalism is like the ethics of human transcendence. Our sense of identity with other human beings overflows and embraces some of our non-human "conscience." Seals, owls and turtles manage to get included. But the farther we go down the evolutionary scale the harder it is for our empathy to stretch. I guess earthworms will just have to look out for themselves. They will have to defend their own world of earthworm beauty.

PEOPLE

I still remember Larry vividly. Larry sat next to me in my Latin class in high school. He was movie-star handsome, a cross between Tyrone Power and John Barrymore. Girls were drawn to him almost immediately. Boys were jealous of his good looks. That is, until he opened his mouth. It wasn't that his voice was intrinsically bad. It was even deep and slightly resonant. But it had an annoying whine to it. Larry always whined. He eternally complained. He articulated every fear that had ever passed through the registry of his mind. He even picked up other people's anxieties and made them his own. Spending any time with Larry was intolerable. He was a talking and walking manifestation of human weakness, indecision and whining dependency. In time even his face and body could not rescue Larry. To know him was to avoid him. Larry was ugly.

I thought of Larry the other day when I met an eighty-year old woman tutoring Russian refugees. She was a little woman with a wrinkled face. At first appearance she almost offended by her looks. One eye was half closed. Her nose was spread all over her face. Her lips were too thick. But she was feisty. Despite her physical frailty she exuded energy. To talk to her was to talk about what she did, not what she feared. She had a strong smile, the kind of smile that says, "I'm glad to be with you, and I have the strength to help you if you need me." Even her posture was different from the posture of most of the women her age that I knew. She held herself straight, a reflection of her determination to look independent. I liked her immediately. She was very appealing. The refugees were attracted to her. Like me, they thought that she was beautiful.

It is very easy to fall into the cliche that outer appearances do not count—that only the inner spirit makes a difference. That is simply not true. Forms and shapes are significant. They are normally connected to our vision of health and vigor. But they are not important enough to transcend a real weakness of the human heart and mind. The beautiful face can be rendered ugly by a mean and fearful psyche. And the ugly face can be turned beautiful by the energy of strength and determination.

A crazy world needs the beauty of strong people. Their presence gives us role models of strength. Noticing them and admiring them is part of our strategy for survival. Some people search the heavens for the most meaningful beauty. I prefer the human scene. Determined old ladies with smiling faces are sometimes as beautiful and as radiant, to me as the sun.

ME

Trying to be good sounds noble. But trying to be beautiful sounds shallow, an adventure in cosmetics and other trivial pursuits. Only vain and self-absorbed people seem to be concerned about their beauty.

Yet that striving for beauty is more important than it seems. Millions of people all over the world want to be beautiful and fail. Millions more are beautiful and do not know that they are. In fact, their not knowing makes them all the more attractive. If beauty is a reflection of the energy of life then it is something more than what cosmetics can produce. We have all seen well-painted faces that are weary with ugliness.

Ed is a neighbor. I see him running every morning. His heart attack and bypass surgery frightened him. He was only forty-eight and the father of two young children when the disaster struck. At the time of the trouble he was fat, lethargic and a chain smoker. He looked older than his age would warrant. He walked like an old man deprived of energy and hope. In fact, I used to think he was very ugly—even though he had well formed and pleasant features. But his despair and surrender were all too obvious. The coronary crisis jolted him out of his self-destruction. He became aware of his mortality and the value of each day that he lived. For the first time in his life he really saw his ugliness and was revolted by what he saw. With the help of his doctor he instituted a new regimen. He dieted. He exercised. He lost weight. The shape of his body began to conform to his new awareness of health. As he established more and more control over his life, self-esteem flowed into his work and family relations. He felt energized and more attractive. When I told him one morning that he was "beautiful," he blushed. But he loved the compliment. And he knew what I meant.

Real beauty requires the training of the will, not paint. Our body and our mind go together. They cannot be separated. Training the body reinforces our will. Training our will gives us the energy of beauty. If we are too deliberate about being beautiful, we will obviously be silly. A little non-awareness will keep us from fatal absorption. But there is nothing wrong about thinking about it from time to time. False humility and self-denial are ugly. They produce the piety of bared heads and prostrate bodies.

The good humor to recognize our limitations is essential to personal beauty. But so is the recognition of our own power.

CONCLUSION

We began with the *grand illusion*. If you do not believe that it is an illusion the message of this book is irrelevant. A meaningful universe will, in the end, make everything in your life turn out alright.

But if you do believe that the grand illusion is indeed an illusion—or if your mind is open to the possibility that it is—then you will recognize that you are living in a crazy world. Living in a crazy world can make you also crazy if you do not defend your sanity.

Defending your sanity is called realism. Realism is the willingness to face the facts as they are—not as we want them to be. It is also the willingness to take them seriously, to let them be the foundation of how we choose to live.

The courage to face facts and not to run away from them is the source of our dignity and self-respect. If we believe that we are cowards, then we cannot admire who we are and what we do. But if we see ourselves as brave enough to confront reality, and not run away, then we feel our strength and become less afraid of what we cannot change.

The path of dignity begins with dismissing the grand illusion. That is the first and hardest step. What follows flows naturally from that decision. We refuse despair and cynicism. We affirm happiness in this mortal life as the only reasonable goal worth pursuing. We tame our hope, our fear, our anger, our love, and our guilt so that our behavior can fit our happiness and the happiness of others. We train ourselves to be strong. We search for the nourishment of beauty. Along the way we discover sanity.

The heart of sanity is *reason*. Reason can function in two

ways—cold and hot. Cold reason is abstract reason, divorced from the tumult of human problems. Hot reason is pragmatic reason, eager to arrange for happiness and survival. Hot reason negotiates with our passions and our desires and offers the compromise which makes life worth living.

Being realistic is being rational. And being rational is being sane. Sane people are always concerned about two things. They are always concerned about their willingness to face the facts. They are always concerned about the consequences of their behavior.

It is not easy to be realistic. It is not only the seductiveness of the grand illusion. It is also the nature of the society in which we presently live.

THE PAST

Traditional religion still dominates much of the world. The grand illusion reigns supreme over many underdeveloped countries. Despite the age of science, fundamentalist religion grows stronger and stronger in the countries where disillusionment with contemporary life is deep. Even in America, the paradigm nation of the modern world, millions of people reject reason and find their comfort in the theology of their pre-modern ancestors.

It is hard to be sane when the norm of a society becomes insanity. We live in a strange world. The most sophisticated research of physicians and psychiatrists exists side by side with doctoral dissertations on why the world is only six thousand years old. Television specials detailing the wonders of the new astronomy are followed by Biblical docudramas purporting to demonstrate that the waters of the Red Sea were indeed divided by some natural or supernatural *fluke*. Press reports about the future of evolution are accompanied by stories about Messianic expectations and the imminent coming of the end of the world and the final judgment.

Despite the bizarre contrasts, realistic people do not despair. They are not surprised—since they are rational. They do not expect that most people will be rational. In fact it is irrational to expect that most people will be rational. One of the facts they learn to live with is that large numbers of people will always be uncomfortable with reason. It is too demanding. It allows too much uncertainty. It acknowledges unpleasant facts. Fundamentalists are simply one of the unpleasant facts realists have to live with. They will not go away. They are a chronic provocation. When they are ambitious and eager for power, they must be resisted. When they are pushy and make outrageous statements in the public media, they must be challenged. When they are quiet and mind their own business and allow realists to mind their own business too, they must be tolerated. Living with them is like living with reality.

THE FUTURE

The world we live in keeps changing very rapidly.

Families are changing. Sexual liberation, feminism and divorce have radically altered the character of the nuclear family. Childless marriages, single mothers, separated parents and homosexual unions are now commonplace. More and more people are either condemned to live alone or choose to live alone.

Work is changing. Jobs for unskilled labor are disappearing. The education and training of one decade becomes obsolete in the next. Work opportunities cross national boundaries and turn the world into an international labor market. Women do the work that once belonged only to men.

Friendship is changing. Needy individuals look for support systems. Friends become family. Women bond intimately with women. Men bond intimately with men. Being a friend invites greater and greater demands.

Technology is changing. Machines are replacing people. Automation advances relentlessly. The human brain alienates more and more of its functions to the computer. Communication is instant.

Politics is changing. The confrontation between East and West turns into the conflict between North and South. The threat of nuclear war shifts to small countries. The United Nations starts to work. Economic unions in Europe and North America change the scope of trade. Democracy becomes increasingly more popular and fragile.

The paralysis of "future shock" is a normal human response to all this change. More and more change means more new consequences. More and more new consequences mean a bigger and bigger headache for reason. Reality is changing so fast that it is hard to keep up with all the facts. The facts no longer have the courtesy to stick around for a long time. Just as we are about to meet them, they turn into something else. It would be so nice to have a few eternal truths to compensate for this relentless change.

But there are no eternal truths. There are simply ever-changing facts. And there is the human mind trying to understand them and human courage trying to live with them. Time will not allow us to master all the facts. But we have more than our own ups and downs. We are social beings. We have human connections. There are billions of eyes and ears. There are billions of human minds struggling to make sense of the changing world.

LIFE OF COURAGE

Choosing the life of courage is not easy. The world we live in is filled with so many risks, so many dangers. The world we have is so different from the world we want. We want a loving and just providence, but it is not there. We want guarantees of happy endings, but they do not exist. We want eternal life, but it is most likely a fantasy. We want stability, but everything is change. We even want to be surrounded by sane and caring people, but they are few and far between.

Choosing cowardice seems so much more attractive. Cowards never have to face the real world. They can invent their own "reality," fill it with whatever they need and want and play make-believe. Yet cowardice exists at its own price. It forces us to lie about our experience. It makes us deny what we see with our own eyes. It humiliates us with our weakness. It exhausts our energy in the battle to resist the truth. It turns us into begging children, grateful for abuse and suffering. It prevents us from assuming responsibility for our own lives. It forces us to negate the one power we do have to cope with, reality, our own power. It makes us as crazy as the world we live in.

The life of courage is hard. But it is, ultimately, rewarding. It makes us pay attention to our own experience. It makes it easy for us to admit the truth. It notices our strength. It protects our dignity. It enable us to assume responsibility for our own lives. It celebrates our own power. It makes us sane in the face of the crazy world.

It even makes us pay attention to the opportunities, as well as the dangers, of the real world. Pleasure is real. Happiness is real. Usefulness is real. Loving and supportive relationships are real. But, if they happen, they are not gifts of destiny. They are human achievements-sometimes against overwhelming odds.

The life of courage rests on the foundation of reason—but it is made out of passion and emotional power. It turns every ordinary day into an extraordinary event of personal resistance and every ordinary person into a hero of determination. As Hannah Arendt, the German Jewish refugee philosopher said, " The connotation of courage, which we now feel to be an indispensable quality of the hero, is, in fact, already present in the willingness to act and speak at all, to insert oneself in the world and begin a story of one's own." (*The Human Condition*)

Realistic living has an heroic touch to it—even for the most nondescript men and women—even in the most pedestrian of settings—because the dangers of failure and death are so real.

Realistic living is the courage to acknowledge the truth, even when it is painful. It is the courage to strive for happiness, even when it is unlikely. It is the courage to make necessary decisions, even when there is uncertainty. It is the courage to improve the world, even in the face of overwhelming defeat. It is, especially, the courage to take both the blame and the credit, even when they are embarrassing.

Realistic living is the courage to stay sane in a crazy world.

The sun requires no courage to rise in the morning, to shine in the day, to "*die*" in the evening. But we—living, breathing, passionate people, we do.

GLOSSARY OF PERSONALITIES

This is a list and description of philosophers. writers and movements mentioned in the text.

AHAD HAAM (Asher Ginsberg) 1856–1927
Russian Jewish Zionist who is the father of "spiritual Zionism." He interpreted the Jewish religious and ethical teachings as expressions of Jewish culture and creativity.

HORATIO ALGER 1834–1899
The most popular author in the United States in the last thirty years of the nineteenth century. His stories were mainly about poor boys who rose from rags to riches.

HANNAH ARENDT 1906–1975
German Jewish intellectual who fled to America during the Hitler era. Her extensive writings explored the sources of totalitarianism, violence, revolution and antisemitism.

DANIEL BELL 1918–
Harvard professor who is one of the leaders of neo-conservative thought in America.

JEREMY BENTHAM 1748–1832
English philosopher who developed the idea that ethical behavior promoted human pleasure. In his eyes right action is the action that produces more significant pleasure than any other action.

HENRI BERGSON 1859–1941

A French philosopher who believed that life's evolution was controlled by a life force which is creative and unpredictable in its effects.

BOETHUIS 480–525

Early Christian theologian and philosopher who tried to demonstrate that reason can be certain about the existence of an omnipotent God and that human freewill is compatible with God's foresight.

WILLIAM F. BUCKLEY 1925–

Acerbic American political writer who is one of the intellectual leaders of the conservative movement in America.

EDMUND BURKE 1729–1797

British politician and writer who was deeply opposed to the excesses of the French Revolution. He sought a balance between freedom and law and order.

JOSEPH CAMPBELL 1904–1987

American mythologist who related mythology to human wisdom. He believed that myths were expressions of an innate knowledge for coping successfully with life, as well as guides to effective spirituality.

ALBERT CAMUS 1913–1960

French writer, born in Algeria, who developed absurdist philosophy and who affirmed the value of life and morality in a meaningless world.

RAM DASS (Richard Alpert) 1931–

American boy turned guru. He became one of the "stars" of the mystical "70's" when Hindu and Buddhist thought attracted a wide following in North America.

JOHN DEWEY 1859–1952

American philosopher who helped to develop the philosophy of pragmatism. He believed that true philosophy helped people solve practical problems.

EMILE DURKHEIM 1858–1917

French intellectual and writer who is regarded as the father of modern sociology.

EPICURUS c. 342–270 B.C.

Greek philosopher who embraced the ideas that reality is material and that the purpose of life is to increase pleasure and to avoid him. For him the highest pleasure was friendship.

FRANCIS FUKUYAMA 1952

Young Japanese-American intellectual who stunned the public with his book, *The End of History*. Fukuyama argues for the ultimate triumph of a liberal capitalism.

SIGMUND FREUD 1856–1939

Austrian neurologist who developed psychoanalysis. He is famous for his exploration of the unconscious mind and its power.

HARE KRISHNA

Hindu sect that has its roots in India and its audience in Europe and North America. The sect reveres the Hindu god Krishna through devotional song and dance and is actively missionary.

GEORGE FRIEDRICH HEGEL 1770–1831

German philosopher who taught at the University of Berlin. He maintained the human history was guided by an intrinsic spirituality and that mind was the foundation of all reality.

THOMAS HOBBES 1588–1679

English philosopher who rejected the supernatural and any supernatural basis for morality. He also believed in the value of authoritarian government.

DAVID HUME 1711–1776

Scottish philosopher and historian who maintained that all thought derives from experience and that there are no innate ideas.

THOMAS JEFFERSON 1743–1826

Third American president and author of the Declaration of Independence. He was also a political philosopher who championed democracy and the separation of religion and government.

JOB

The hero of a book in the Bible who refused to repudiate God because of unjust suffering.

IMMANUEL KANT 1724–1804

German philosopher and rationalist who denied the possibility of knowing anything beyond our experience and who maintained that it was impossible to prove either the existence or non-existence of God.

FRANZ KAFKA 1883–1928

Austrian Jewish novelist who dramatized the dilemma of living in an unjust and unresponsive universe. His home was Prague and he wrote in German.

WALTER KAUFMAN 1921–1980

American philosopher and Princeton professor who explored the connections between philosophy and religion. He invented the word "decidophobia," the fear of making decisions or of being responsible for them.

MORDECAI KAPLAN 1881–1983

Lithuanian born American rabbi who was the founder and intellectual guide of Reconstructionist Judaism. Deeply influenced by both John Dewey and Emile Durkheim, he sought to redefine Judaism in a naturalistic way.

ARTHUR KOESTLER 1905–1983

Hungarian born journalist and writer who broke with Communism and who gave dramatic expression to his disillusionment.

IRVING KRISTOL 1920–

American writer who abandoned his Marxist views to become a champion of capitalism. He is one of the leading intellectuals of the neo-conservative movement who has become disillusioned with rationality.

HAROLD KUSHNER 1935–

American rabbi who wrote, *When Bad Things Happen To Good People*. He was deeply influenced by Mordecai Kaplan and accepted Kaplan's redefinition of God as a non-supernatural all-good limited force.

GOTTFRIED LEIBNIZ 1646–1716

German philosopher and mathematician who helped to develop differential and integral calculus. He resisted the idea that the universe was composed of only material atoms.

LYNDON LA ROUCHE 1922–

Controversial American political figure who is the leader of the American Labor Party. He embraces a conspirational view of human history which seems to be under the control of both the Queen of England and the Zionists.

KARL MARX 1818–1883

German philosopher who is the author of dialectal materialism. He viewed human history as a drama of class conflict which would ultimately resolve itself in the last revolution and in the utopia of a classless egalitarian communism.

MARY, QUEEN OF SCOTS 1542–1587

Queen of Scotland who defended her Catholic faith against Protestant John Knox and who was beheaded by order of Queen Elizabeth of England.

JOHN STUART MILL 1806–1873

English philosopher who became the articulate spokesman for a classical liberalism, which found its roots in reason, personal freedom and naturalism.

MIND CONTROL

The Jose' Silva movement of Mind Control sought in the 1970's to train people to control their body and their environment through mental relaxation. The results were generally less spectacular than advertised, what with claims to clairvoyant power.

MOONIES

A nickname for the followers of Reverend Moon, a Korean religious leader who maintains that he is a Christian and also a divine figure like Jesus. The sect is both wealthy and aggressive.

MUKTANANDA 1908–1982

Founder of the Shree Gurudev Siddha Yoga Ashram in California. Swami Muktananda Paramahansa sought to awaken divine consciousness in his disciples by a subtle spiritual process of transmission. Freedom from suffering and supreme bliss were among the goals of the ashram.

ISAAC NEWTON 1642–1727

English scientist who developed the idea of a universe of infinite space, which featured the power of gravity and was governed by the inexorable laws of nature which not even God could abolish.

FRIEDRICH NIETZSCHE 1844–1900

German philosopher who is the author of the phrase "God is dead." Nietzsche believed that the old Christian morality was bankrupt and needed to be replaced by a new ethics which glorified human power and will.

JOSE ORTEGA Y GASSETT 1883–1955

Spanish philosopher who predicted that the forces of democracy would ultimately be overwhelmed by the dark powers of totalitarianism.

FRITZ PERLS 1904–1970

American psychologist who helped to develop *gestalt* psychology and who was one of the leading figures of the Vietnam era spirituality. His home base was the Esalen Institute.

NORMAN PODHORETZ 1930–

American Jewish intellectual who is editor of *Commentary* magazine. A former Trotskyite, he became one of the leaders of the neo-conservative movement together with Daniel Bell and Irving Kristol.

PROTAGORAS c.485–411 B.C.

Greek philosopher who was the antagonist of Socrates and Plato. He did not believe in the gods and he maintained that "man is the measure of all things."

AYN RAND 1905–1984

American philosopher, playwright and novelist who turned ethics upside down by maintaining the virtue of selfishness. She called her philosophy Objectivism.

JEAN-JACQUES ROUSSEAU 1712–1778

Swiss philosopher who was one of the precursors of the Romantic movement. He believed that human institutions corrupt human nature and that natural feeling is superior to reason.

GEORGE SANTAYANA 1863–1952

American philosopher of Spanish origin who sought to combine a realistic and naturalistic view of the world with the cultivation of beauty and aesthetic imagination.

JEAN-PAUL SARTRE 1905–1980

French philosopher, novelist and playwright who helped to create popular existentialism. A hero of the Resistance, he exalted human freedom and human responsibility in a harsh setting where the universe had no moral agenda.

ARTHUR SCHOPENHAUER 1788–1860
German philosopher who saw at the heart of the universe a blind and mindless will. His pessimism ultimately led to his suicide.

SCIENTOLOGY
A religion and a psychotherapy invented by enterprising Ron Hubbard who first called it *Dianetics.* Hubbard maintained that present anxiety and neurosis were related not only to events in our present-life but to traumas in our previous lives.

GEORGE BERNARD SHAW 1856–1950
Eccentric English playwright who became England's most famous theater figure. Like Henri Bergson, Shaw believed in a life force that infused the course of human history and gave it direction.

SOCRATES c. 469–399 B.C.
Greek philosopher and mentor of Plato, who was put to death by the government of Athens for corrupting morals. He was a devotee of reason who was fearless in his assaults on tradition.

BARUCH SPINOZA 1632–1677
Dutch philosopher of Portugese Jewish origin who suffered public rejection and religious excommunication in order to espouse his pantheistic view of God and his love of personal freedom.

VOLTAIRE (Francis Marie Arouet) 1694–1778
French essayist and philosopher who was the intellectual darling of his

age. While his rational view of the world outraged the Church, it found a welcoming ear among the skeptical aristocracy and rising bourgeoisie.

WALT WHITMAN 1819–1892

American poet who sought to create a unique American style of poetry. His poetry reflects his optimism and his ardent poetry.

ZENO 334–262 B.C.

Greek philosopher from Cyprus who established the Stoic school in Athens. Stoicism was an austere discipline which taught its followers to behave ethically with no prospect of personal reward.